MACBETH

WILLIAM SHAKESPEARE

edited by
Oscar James Campbell

CHARTS AND MAPS

AUTHOR BIOGRAPHY

COMPLETE BACKGROUND

CAPSULE SUMMARY

COMPREHENSIVE SUMMARY

CRITICAL ANALYSIS

CHARACTER ANALYSIS

QUESTIONS AND ANSWERS

ORIGINAL TEXT

BIBLIOGRAPHY

GLOSSARY

MACBETH
WILLIAM SHAKESPEARE

with an

analytical interpretation

by

PAUL N. SIEGEL, Ph.D.

Editorial Consultant

John T. Shawcross
Professor of English
University of Wisconsin

Time Machine Classics

DIVISION OF INFORMATION INCORPORATED

New York, New York

THE AUTHOR: Paul N. Siegel received his M.A. and Ph.D. from Harvard University, his B.S. from City College of New York. He has taught at the University of Connecticut, City College of New York, Ripon College, and since 1956 has been Professor and Chairman of the English Department at Long Island University. A former recipient of the Ford Foundation Fund for the Advancement of Education to study the history of Renaissance England, Dr. Siegel has acted as editorial consultant on Shakespeare manuscripts to PMLA and to University of Kentucky Press. Member of the Columbia University Seminar in the Renaissance, Shakespeare Association of America, Renaissance Society of America, MLA, NCTE, and AAUP, he has acted as Secretary and Chairman of the Renaissance Group of the Modern Language Association.

Dr. Siegel, internationally recognized Shakespearean critic, is the author of *Shakespearean Tragedy and the Elizabethan Compromise* (New York University Press, 1957) and *His Infinite Variety: Major Shakespearean Criticism since Johnson* (Lippincott, 1964). His numerous articles, notes, and reviews have appeared in such periodicals as *Shakespeare Quarterly, Philological Quarterly, Studies in Philology, Shakespeare Newsletter, Modern Language Notes, College English, Explicator*, and *Renaissance News*. His *Shakespeare in His Time and Ours* will be published soon by the University of Notre Dame Press.

PREFACE

Classics are works that are "not for an age, but for all time." The great wealth of vital knowledge inherent in the classics is as relevant today as it was when the books were written. Much that is significant, even crucial and indispensable to a complete understanding of contemporary life, escapes the person who has not been provided with a foundation in the classics.

Because language changes in idiom and vocabulary, and because the author's frame of reference undergoes a more or less thorough transformation with the passing years, the original text of a work begins to grow archaic and to become increasingly inaccessible to later readers. Thus, a communication gap develops. Without a competent guide, the reader may wander in circles forever in the unmarked forest. Even more tragic, he may not realize that he is lost.

While profound studies of the classics abound, they are usually written in esoteric technical language by scholars to impress other scholars. The general reader may well say, as Byron said of Coleridge, "I wish he would explain his explanation!" The great advantage of T. M. Classics is that the guides, while written by eminent scholars, are directed not to a special audience of scholars, but to the general reader.

Of course, the classic itself is the focus; nothing can be a substitute for reading the text itself. A classic is a work of original genius, a distillation of the thinking of one of the great minds in human history while it was at one of its peaks. Just as no verbal description of a symphony can substitute for hearing the music itself, likewise no description of a classic can convey its essence, its perspective, its manner and tone, its sound and feel. One of the greatest advantages of T. M. Classics is that they include every word of the original. Not a single fact or idea, not a single implication or nuance gets lost.

T. M. Classics have made the unique riches of the world's greatest works accessible to the general reader, in full original texts, without alteration, without distortion, without diminution; and these texts are accompanied by expert guides carefully oriented to the needs of the general reader. This is why T. M. Classics represent a major breakthrough in a universal understanding of the great works of literature. As such, they belong in the home of every thinking American.

Paul Smith, Ph.D.
Harvard University

CONTENTS

SHAKESPEARE'S
BRITAIN
KEY
MAP
INVERNESS
FORRES
BIRNAM WOOD
DUNSINANE
HOLMEDON
WARKWORTH
CASTLE
CARLISLE
ISLE OF
MAN
MIDDLEHAM
CASTLE
GAULTREE FOREST
TOWTON
YORK
WAKEFIELD
POMFRET CASTLE
SANDAL CASTLE
DONCASTER
BANGOR
FLINT
CASTLE
BARKLOUGHLY CASTLE
LINCOLN
SHREWSBURY
SWINSTEAD
ABBEY
BRIDGENORTH
TAMWORTH
BOSWORTH FIELD
LEICESTER
LUDLOW
COVENTRY
MORTIMER'S CROSS
KENILWORTH
ELY
MILFORD HAVEN
WORCESTER
WARWICK
KIMBOLTON
STRATFORD
BURY ST. EDMUNDS
MONMOUTH
TEWKESBURY
CAMBRIDGE
GLOUCESTER
OXFORD
ST. ALBANS
BRISTOL
STAINES
LONDON
DARTFORD
SALISBURY
GADSHILL
CANTERBURY
EXETER
WINCHESTER
ROCHESTER
SOUTHAMPTON
DOVER
CALAIS
AGINCOURT
created for
EDUCATIONAL
RESEARCH
ASSOCIATES, INC.
of America
EXCLUSIVELY
ERA
HARFLEUR
PARIS
ORLEANS

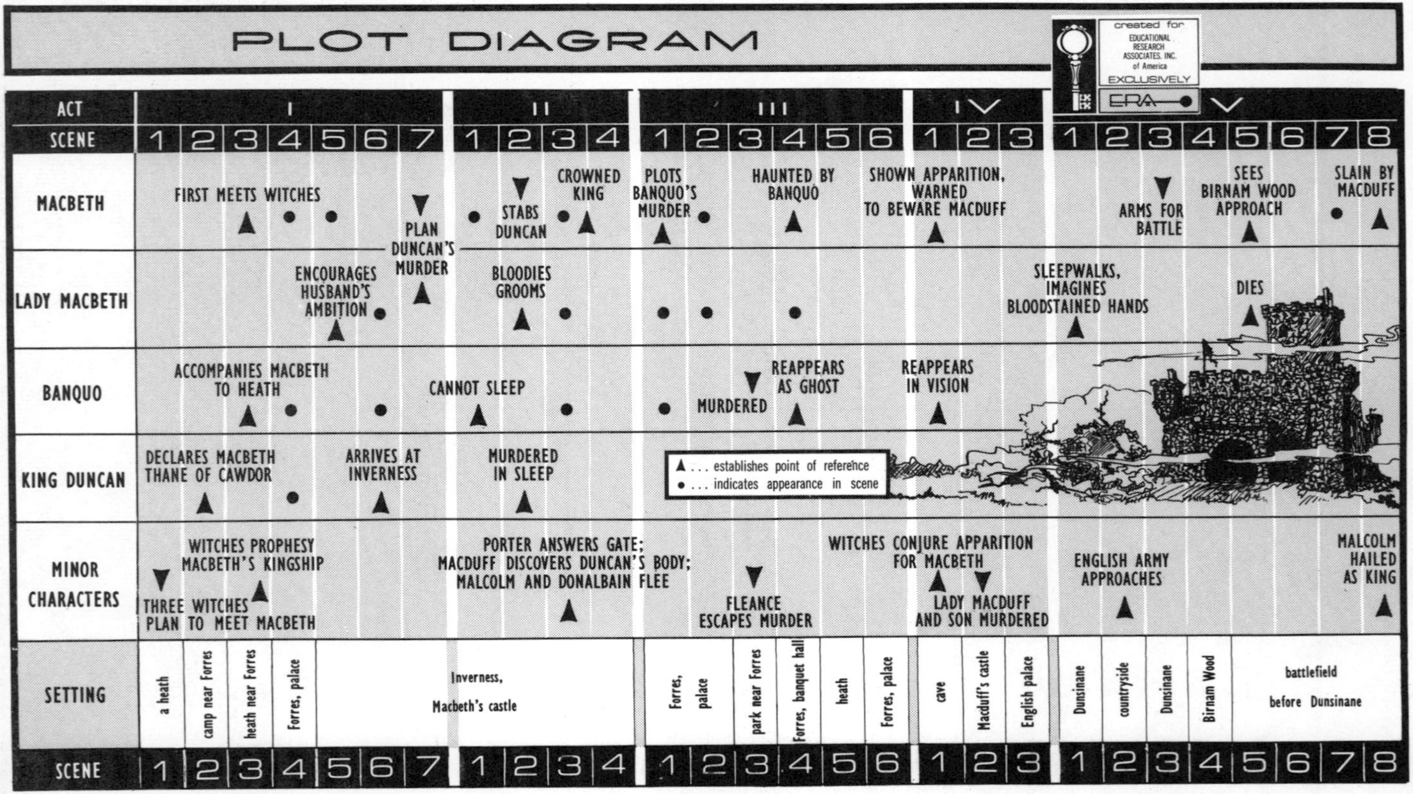

PLOT DIAGRAM

created for EDUCATIONAL RESEARCH ASSOCIATES, INC. of America EXCLUSIVELY ERA

ACT	I						
SCENE	1	2	3	4	5	6	7
MACBETH			▲ FIRST MEETS WITCHES	●	●		▼ PLAN DUNCAN'S MURDER
LADY MACBETH					▲ ENCOURAGES HUSBAND'S AMBITION	●	▲
BANQUO			▲ ACCOMPANIES MACBETH TO HEATH	●		●	
KING DUNCAN		▲ DECLARES MACBETH THANE OF CAWDOR		●		▲ ARRIVES AT INVERNESS	
MINOR CHARACTERS	▼ THREE WITCHES PLAN TO MEET MACBETH		▲ WITCHES PROPHESY MACBETH'S KINGSHIP				
SETTING	a heath	camp near Forres	heath near Forres	Forres, palace	Inverness, Macbeth's castle		

ACT	II			
SCENE	1	2	3	4
MACBETH	●	▼ STABS DUNCAN	●	▲ CROWNED KING
LADY MACBETH		▲ BLOODIES GROOMS	●	
BANQUO	▲ CANNOT SLEEP		●	
KING DUNCAN		▲ MURDERED IN SLEEP		
MINOR CHARACTERS			▲ PORTER ANSWERS GATE; MACDUFF DISCOVERS DUNCAN'S BODY; MALCOLM AND DONALBAIN FLEE	
SETTING	Inverness, Macbeth's castle			

ACT	III					
SCENE	1	2	3	4	5	6
MACBETH	▲ PLOTS BANQUO'S MURDER	●		▲ HAUNTED BY BANQUO		
LADY MACBETH	●	●		●		
BANQUO	●		▼ MURDERED	▲ REAPPEARS AS GHOST		
KING DUNCAN						
MINOR CHARACTERS			▼ FLEANCE ESCAPES MURDER			
SETTING	Forres, palace		park near Forres	Forres, banquet hall	heath	Forres, palace

ACT	IV		
SCENE	1	2	3
MACBETH	▲ SHOWN APPARITION, WARNED TO BEWARE MACDUFF		
LADY MACBETH			
BANQUO	▲ REAPPEARS IN VISION		
KING DUNCAN			
MINOR CHARACTERS	▲ WITCHES CONJURE APPARITION FOR MACBETH	▼ LADY MACDUFF AND SON MURDERED	
SETTING	cave	Macduff's castle	English palace

ACT	V							
SCENE	1	2	3	4	5	6	7	8
MACBETH			▼ ARMS FOR BATTLE		▲ SEES BIRNAM WOOD APPROACH		●	▲ SLAIN BY MACDUFF
LADY MACBETH	▲ SLEEPWALKS, IMAGINES BLOODSTAINED HANDS				▲ DIES			
BANQUO								
KING DUNCAN								
MINOR CHARACTERS		▲ ENGLISH ARMY APPROACHES						▲ MALCOLM HAILED AS KING
SETTING	Dunsinane	countryside	Dunsinane	Birnam Wood	battlefield before Dunsinane			

▲ . . . establishes point of reference
● . . . indicates appearance in scene

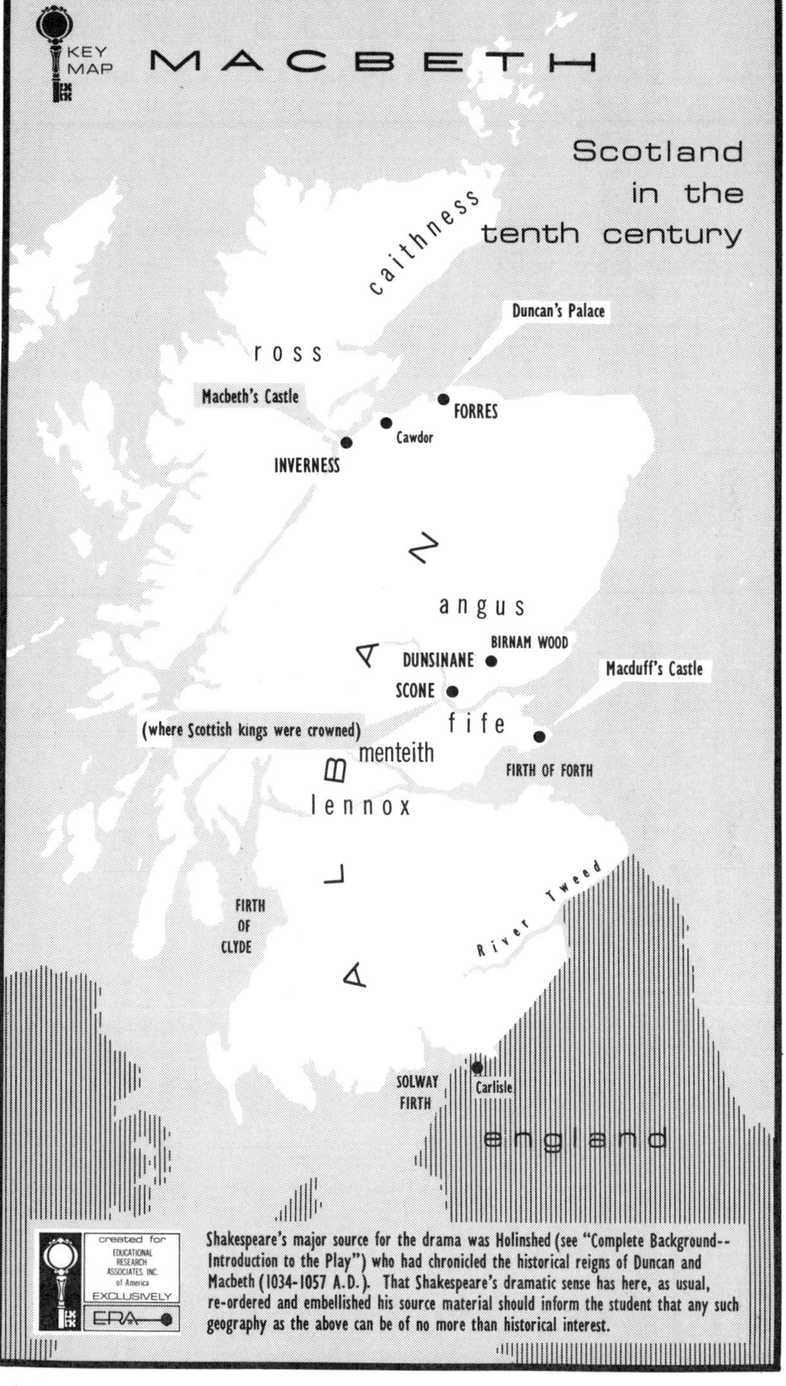

Shakespeare's major source for the drama was Holinshed (see "Complete Background--Introduction to the Play") who had chronicled the historical reigns of Duncan and Macbeth (1034-1057 A.D.). That Shakespeare's dramatic sense has here, as usual, re-ordered and embellished his source material should inform the student that any such geography as the above can be of no more than historical interest.

WILLIAM SHAKESPEARE

BIOGRAPH

DATE		AGE	BIOGRAPHIC HIGHLIGHTS	CONTEMPORARY EVENTS		LITERARY EVENTS	
1564	Apr. 23		PROBABLE BIRTH DATE, STRATFORD			"The Theatre" and "The Curtain" opened	1576, 1577
	Apr. 26		BAPTIZED, HOLY TRINITY CHURCH	ELIZABETH I, QUEEN OF ENGLAND	1558		
1582	Nov. 27	19	MARRIAGE LICENSE ISSUED (ANNE WHATELY)	MARY OF SCOTLAND DETHRONED	1567	HOLINSHED, Chronicles	1577
	Nov. 28		MARRIAGE BOND SIGNED (ANNE HATHAWAY)	DRAKE CIRCUMNAVIGATES THE WORLD	1576	THE QUEEN'S COMPANY FORMED	1583
1583	May 26	20	DAUGHTER SUSANNA BAPTIZED	DEFEAT OF THE SPANISH ARMADA	1588		
1585	Feb. 2	21	SON AND DAUGHTER HAMNET AND JUDITH BAPTIZED	HENRY IV BECOMES KING OF FRANCE	1589		
1592		28	RESIDING IN LONDON; REFERRED TO IN PRINT BY ROBERT GREENE AND HENRY CHETTLE	ENGLAND MISTRESS OF HIGH SEAS; DECADE OF RELATIVE PROSPERITY; THERE ARE POLITICAL AND RELIGIOUS UNCERTAINTIES, HOWEVER, AS TO THE FUTURE OF THE THRONE AT THE DEATH OF THE "VIRGIN QUEEN."		SPENSER, Faerie Queene I-III	1590
1593	Apr. 19	29	"VENUS AND ADONIS" REGISTERED; THEN PUBLISHED			MARLOWE, Dr. Faustus	1593
1594	May 9	30	"RAPE OF LUCRECE" REGISTERED; THEN PUBLISHED			THEATERS CLOSED BY PLAGUE	1593
	Dec. 28		PERFORMANCE, "COMEDY OF ERRORS" AT GRAY'S INN				
1595	Mar. 15	30	PAID AS MEMBER OF LORD CHAMBERLAIN'S MEN				
1596	Aug. 11	32	SON HAMNET BURIED, STRATFORD			SPENSER, Faerie Queene IV-VI	1596
	Oct. 20		FATHER GIVEN HERALDIC ARMS				
1597	May 4	33	PURCHASED NEW PLACE, STRATFORD			BACON, Essays	1597
	Aug. 29		"RICHARD II" REGISTERED; THEN PUBLISHED	EDICT OF NANTES	1598		
1598		34	FIRST USE OF NAME ON TITLE PAGE	ELIZABETHAN POOR LAW	1601	GLOBE THEATER BUILT	1599
			ACTED IN JONSON'S "EVERY MAN IN HIS HUMOUR"	JAMES I SUCCEEDS QUEEN ELIZABETH	1603	CERVANTES, Don Quixote I	1605
1603		39	COMPANY BECOMES KINGS MEN	IRISH REVOLT SUPPRESSED	1603	BACON, Advancement of Learning	1605
1609	May 20	45	"SONNETS" REGISTERED; THEN PUBLISHED	GUNPOWDER PLOT	1605	The Douai Old Testament	1609
1613		49	BUYS HOME IN BLACKFRIARS	JAMESTOWN FOUNDED	1607	King James Bible	1611
1616	Apr. 23	52	APPARENT DATE OF DEATH	"THIRTY YEARS WAR" BEGINS	1618	DEATH OF CERVANTES	1616
	Apr. 25		BURIED HOLY TRINITY CHURCH, STRATFORD			JONSON, Folio Edition of Poems	1616
1623			MONUMENT ERECTED AT STRATFORD; ANNE HATHAWAY DIES; "FIRST FOLIO" PUBLISHED	PILGRIMS SETTLE IN NEW ENGLAND	1620	BURTON, Anatomy of Melancholy	1621
						DONNE, Devotions	1624

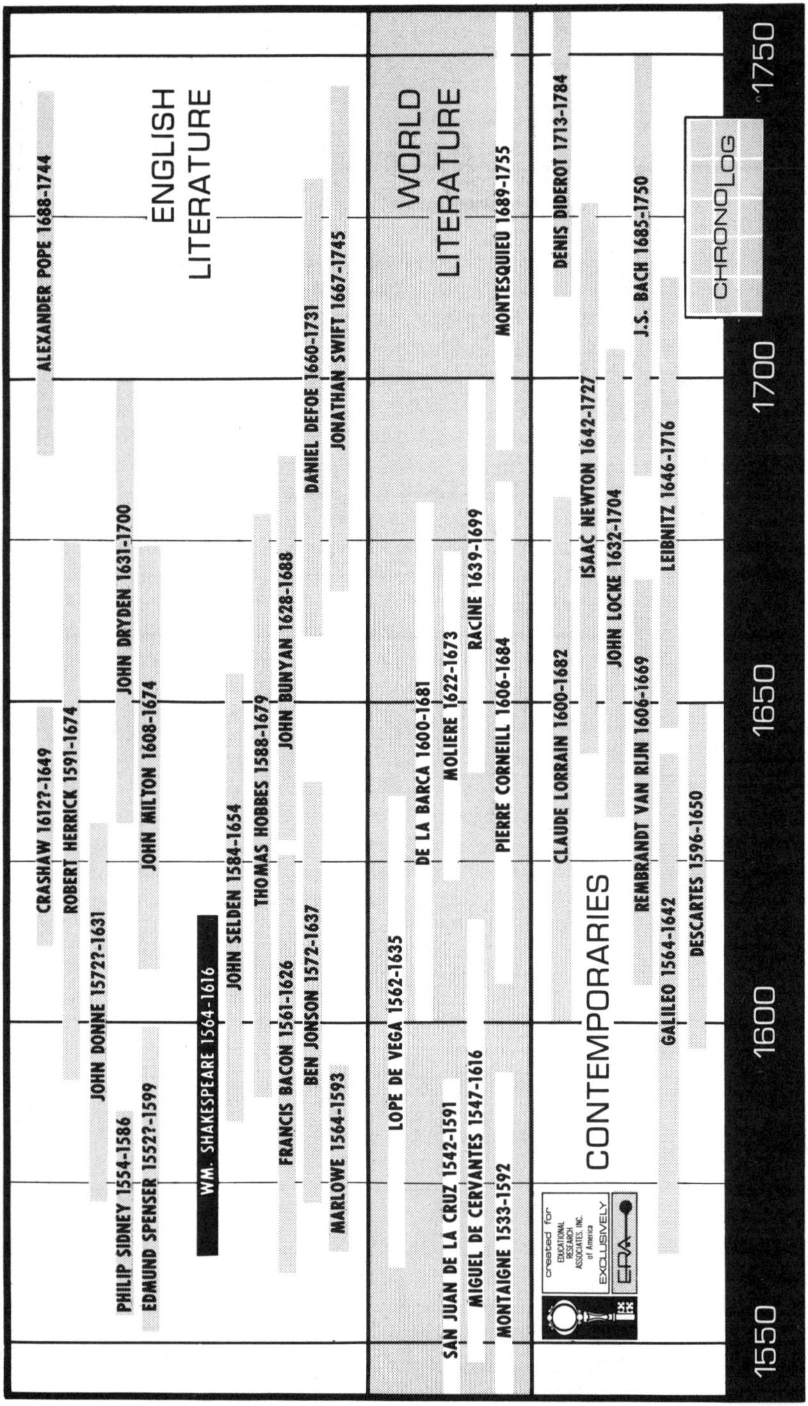

ENGLISH LITERATURE

CRASHAW 1612?-1649
ALEXANDER POPE 1688-1744
ROBERT HERRICK 1591-1674
JOHN DONNE 1572?-1631
PHILIP SIDNEY 1554-1586
JOHN DRYDEN 1631-1700
EDMUND SPENSER 1552?-1599
JOHN MILTON 1608-1674
WM. SHAKESPEARE 1564-1616
JOHN SELDEN 1584-1654
THOMAS HOBBES 1588-1679
FRANCIS BACON 1561-1626
JOHN BUNYAN 1628-1688
BEN JONSON 1572-1637
DANIEL DEFOE 1660-1731
MARLOWE 1564-1593
JONATHAN SWIFT 1667-1745

WORLD LITERATURE

LOPE DE VEGA 1562-1635
DE LA BARCA 1600-1681
SAN JUAN DE LA CRUZ 1542-1591
MOLIERE 1622-1673
MIGUEL DE CERVANTES 1547-1616
RACINE 1639-1699
MONTAIGNE 1533-1592
PIERRE CORNEILL 1606-1684
MONTESQUIEU 1689-1755

CONTEMPORARIES

CLAUDE LORRAIN 1600-1682
DENIS DIDEROT 1713-1784
ISAAC NEWTON 1642-1727
JOHN LOCKE 1632-1704
REMBRANDT VAN RIJN 1606-1669
J.S. BACH 1685-1750
GALILEO 1564-1642
LEIBNITZ 1646-1716
DESCARTES 1596-1650

1550 1600 1650 1700 1750

created for EDUCATIONAL RESEARCH ASSOCIATES, INC. of America EXCLUSIVELY ERA

CHRONOLOG

ELIZABETHAN THEATER
a composite representation
A
B
C
D
D
E
E
F
G
H
J
K
L
M
N
A. HUT, to house prop machinery
B. TOP STAGE, primarily music gallery
C. STORAGE LOFTS and DRESSING ROOMS
D. GENTLEMEN'S ROOMS (LORD'S ROOMS)
E. WINDOW STAGES
F. UPPER STAGE
G. DRESSING ROOMS
H. INNER STAGE
J. TRAP DOORS
K. BACK STAGE AREA
L. MAIN ENTRANCE
M. OUTER STAGE
N. PIT
created for
EDUCATIONAL
RESEARCH
ASSOCIATES, INC.
of America
EXCLUSIVELY
ERA

WILLIAM SHAKESPEARE

Biographical Sketch

With the epithet "Dear Son of Memory," Milton praised Shakespeare as one constantly in our memories and brother of the Muses. Certainly no other author has held such sway over the literary world, undiminished through some three and a half centuries of shifting artistic tastes. Shakespeare's plots and his characters have continued to be a living reality for us; as his well-known contemporary Ben Jonson wrote, in a familiar tribute, "Thou . . . art alive still, while thy Booke doth live, / And we have wits to read, and praise to give."

The Early Years Despite such acclaim and the scholarship it has spawned, our knowledge of Shakespeare's life is sketchy, filled with more questions than answers, even after we prune away the misinformation accumulated over the years. He was baptized on April 26, 1564, in Holy Trinity Church, Stratford-on-Avon. As it was customary to baptize children a few days after birth, we conjecture that he was born on April 23. The monument erected in Stratford states that he died on April 23, 1616, in his fifty-third year.

William was the third child of John Shakespeare, who came to Stratford from Snitterfield before 1532 as a "whyttawer" (tanner) and glover, and Mary Arden, daughter of a wealthy "gentleman of worship" from Wilmecote. They married around 1557. Since John Shakespeare owned one house on Greenhill Street and two on Henley Street, we cannot be certain where William was born, though the Henley Street shrine draws many tourists each year. William's two older sisters died in infancy, but three brothers and two sisters survived at least into childhood.

Shakespeare's father was fairly well-to-do, dealing in farm products and wool, and owning considerable property in Stratford. After holding a series of minor municipal offices he was elected alderman in 1565, high baliff (roughly similar to the mayor of today) in 1568, and chief alderman in 1571. There are no records of young Will Shakespeare's education (though there are many unfounded legends), but he undoubtedly attended the town school maintained by the burgesses, which prepared its students for the universities. Ben Jonson's line about Shakespeare's having "small *Latine,* and lesse *Greeke*" refers not to his education but to his lack of indebtedness to the classical writers and dramatists.

On November 28, 1582, a license to marry was issued to "Willelmum Shaxpere *et* Annam Whateley *de* Temple Gratfon," and on the next day a marriage bond for "Willm Shagspere" and "Anne Hathwey of Stratford" was signed by Fulk Sandells and John Richardson, farmers of Stratford. This bond stated that there was no "lawful let or impediment by reason of any precontract, consanguinity, affinity, or by any other lawful means whatsoever"; thus "William and Anne [were] to be married together with once asking of the banns of matrimony." The problem of Anne Whateley has led many researchers and some detractors to argue all kinds of improbabilities, such as the existence of two different Shakespeares and the forging of documents to conceal Shakespeare's true identity. The actual explanation seems to be simple: the clerk who made the marriage license entry apparently copied the name "Whateley" from a preceding entry, as a glance at the full sheet suggests. (Incidentally, Nicholas Rowe in his life of Shakespeare, published in 1709, well before the discovery of these marriage records, gave Anne's name as Hathaway.) The problems of marriage with Anne Hathaway—he was eighteen and she was twenty-six—and of the bond have caused similar consternation. Why did these two marry when there was such a discrepancy of age? Why only one saying of the banns (rather than the usual three)? Why the emphasis on a possible legal impediment? The answer here is not simple or definite, but the birth of a daughter Susanna, baptized at Holy Trinity on May 26, 1583, seems to explain the odd circumstances. However, it should be recognized that an engagement to marry was considered legally binding in those days (we still have breach-of-promise suits today) and that premarital relations were not unusual or frowned upon when an engagement had taken place. The circumstances already mentioned, Shakespeare's ensuing activities, and his will bequeathing to Anne "my second best bed with the furniture" have suggested to some that their marriage was not entirely happy. Their other children, the twins Hamnet and Judith, were christened on February 2, 1585.

Theatrical Life Shakespeare's years before and immediately after the time of his marriage are not charted, but rumor has him as an apprentice to a master butcher or as a country teacher or an actor with some provincial company. He is supposed to have run away from whatever he was doing for livelihood and to have gone to London, where he soon attached himself to some theatrical group. At this time there were only two professional houses established in the London environs. The Theatre (opened in 1576) and The Curtain (opened in 1577). His first connection with the theater was reputedly as holder of horses; that is, one of the stage crew, but a most inferior assignment. Thereafter he became an actor (perhaps at this time he met Ben Jonson), a writer, and a director. Such experience had its mark in the theatricality of his plays. We do know that he was established in London by 1592, when Robert Greene lamented in *A Groats-worth of Wit* (September 1592) that professional actors had gained priority in the theater over university-trained writers like himself: "There is an upstart Crow, beautified with our feathers, that with his *Tygers hart wrapt in a Players hyde,* supposes he is as well able to bombast out a blanke verse as the best of you: and beeing an absolute *Iohannes fac totum* [Jack-of-all-trades], is in his owne conceit the onely Shake-scene in a countrey." An apology for Greene's ill-humored statement by Henry Chettle, the editor of the pamphlet, appeared around December 1592 in *Kind-Hart's Dream.*

Family Affairs To return to the known details of family life, Shakespeare's son Hamnet was buried at Stratford on August 11, 1596; his father was given a coat of arms on October 20, 1596; and he purchased New Place (a refurbished tourist attraction today) on May 4, 1597. The London playwright obviously had not severed connections with his birthplace, and he was reflecting his new affluence by being known as William Shakespeare of Stratford-upon-Avon, in the County of Warwick, Gentleman. His father was buried in Stratford on September 8, 1601; his mother, on September 9, 1608. His daughter Susanna married Dr. John Hall on June 5, 1607, and they had a child named Elizabeth. His other daughter, Judith, married Thomas Quiney on February 10, 1616, without special license, during Lent and was thus excommunicated. Shakespeare revised his will on March 25, 1616, and was buried on April 25, 1616 (according to the parish register). A monument by Gerard Janssen was erected in the Holy Trinity chancel in 1623, but many, like Milton seven years later, protested:

What needs my *Shakespear* for his honour'd Bones,
The labour of an age in piled Stones, . . .
Thou in our wonder and astonishment
Hast built thy self a live-long Monument.

Shakespeare's Writings

Order of Appearance Dating of Shakespeare's early plays, while based on inconclusive evidence, has tended to hover around the early 1590's. Almost certainly it is his chronicles of Henry the Sixth that Philip Henslowe, an important theatrical manager of the day, referred to in his diary as being performed during March-May 1592. An allusion to these plays also occurs in Thomas Nashe's *Piers Penniless His Supplication to the Devil* (August 1592). Greene's quotation about a tiger is a paraphrase of 'O tiger's heart wrapt in a woman's hide" from *3 Henry VI* (I,iv,137).

The first published work to come from Shakespeare's hand was *Venus and Adonis* (1593), a long stanzaic poem, dedicated to Henry Wriothesley, Earl of Southampton. A year later *The Rape of Lucrece* appeared, also dedicated to Southampton. Perhaps poetry was pursued during these years because the London theaters were closed as a result of a virulent siege of plague. The *Sonnets,* published in 1609, may owe something to Southampton, who had become Shakespeare's patron. Perhaps some were written as early as the first few years of the 1590's. They were mentioned (along with a number of plays) in 1598 by Francis Meres in his *Palladis Tamia,* and sonnets 138 and 144 were printed without authority by William Jaggard in *The Passionate Pilgrim* (1599).

There is a record of a performance of *A Comedy of Errors* at Gray's Inn (one of the law colleges) on December 28, 1594, and during early 1595, Shakespeare was paid, along with the famous actors Richard Burbage and William Kempe, for performances before the Queen by the Lord Chamberlain's Men, a theatrical company formed the year before. The company founded the Globe Theater on the south side of the Thames in 1599 and became the King's Men when James ascended the throne. Records show frequent payments to the company through its general manager John Heminge. From 1595 through 1614 there are numerous references to real estate transactions and other legal matters, to many performances, and to various publications connected with Shakespeare.

Order of Publication The first plays to be printed were *Titus Andronicus* around February 1594, and the garbled versions of *Henry VI,* Parts 2 and 3 in the same year. (Some scholars maintain that these last two are early versions of the *Henry VI* plays that appeared in 1596; others feel that they are completely different plays and deny Shakespeare's authorship of the 1594 *Henry VI* plays altogether.) Thereafter *Richard III* appeared in 1597 and 1598; *Richard II,* in 1597 and twice in 1598; *Romeo and Juliet,* in 1597 (a pirated edition) and 1599; and many others. Some of the plays appear in individual editions, with or without Shakespeare's name on the title page; but eighteen are known only from their appearance in the first collected

SHAKESPEARE'S PLAYS

Exact dates for Shakespeare's plays remain a source of debate among scholars. The following serve only as a general frame of reference.

DATE	COMEDIES	TRAGEDIES	HISTORIES
1591			1 Henry VI
1592	Comedy of Errors		2 Henry VI
	Two Gentlemen		3 Henry VI
1593	Love's Labours Lost	Titus Andronicus	Richard III
1594			King John
1595	Midsummer-Night's Dream	Romeo and Juliet	Richard II
1596	Merchant of Venice		
	Taming of the Shrew		
1597			1 Henry IV
1598	Much Ado		2 Henry IV
1599	As You Like It	Julius Caesar	
	Merry Wives		Henry V
1601	Twelfth Night	Hamlet	
1602	Troilus and Cressida		
	All's Well		
1604	Measure for Measure	Othello	
1605		King Lear	
1606		Macbeth	
1607		Timon of Athens	
		Antony and Cleopatra	
1608	Pericles		
1609		Coriolanus	
1610	Cymbeline		
1611	Winter's Tale		
	Tempest		
1613			Henry VIII

volume (the so-called First Folio) of 1623. The editors were Heminge and Henry Condell, another member of Shakespeare's company. *Pericles* was omitted from the First Folio although it had appeared in 1609, 1611, and 1619; it was added to the Third Folio in 1664.

There was reluctance to publish plays at this time for various reasons: many plays were carelessly written for fast production; collaboration was frequent; plays were not really considered *reading* matter; they were sometimes circulated in manuscript; and the theatrical company, not the author, owned the rights. Those plays given individual publication appeared in a quarto, so named from the size of the page. A single sheet of paper was folded twice to make four leaves (thus *quarto*) or eight pages; these four leaves constitute one signature (one section of a bound book). A page measures about 6¾ in. x 8½ in. On the other hand, a folio sheet is folded once to make two leaves or four pages; three sheets, or twelve pages, constitute a signature. The page is approximately 8½ in. x 13⅜ in.

Authorized publication occurred when a company disbanded, when money was needed but rights were to be retained, when a play failed or ran into licensing difficulties (thus hopefully the printed work would justify the play against the criticism), or when a play had been pirated. Authorized editions are called good quartos. Piratical publication might occur when the manuscript of a play had circulated privately, when a member of a company desired money for himself, or when a stenographer or memorizer took the play down in the theater (such a version was recognizable by inclusion of stage directions derived from an eyewitness, by garbled sections, etc.). Pirated editions are called bad quartos; there are at least five bad quartos of Shakespeare's plays.

Authenticity of Works Usually thirty-seven plays are printed in modern collections of Shakespeare's works, but some recent scholars have urged the addition of two more: *Edward III* and *Two Noble Kinsmen.* A case has also been advanced, unconvincingly, for a fragment of a play on Sir Thomas More. At times six of the generally accepted plays have been questioned: *Henry VI*, Parts 1, 2 and 3, *Timon of Athens, Pericles,* and *Henry VIII.* The first four are usually accepted today (one hopes all question concerning *Timon* has finally ended), but if Shakespeare did not write these six plays in their entirety, he certainly wrote parts of them. Of course, collaboration in those days was commonplace. Aside from the two long narrative poems already mentioned and the sonnets (Nos. 1-152, but not Nos. 153-154), Shakespeare's poetic output is uncertain. *The Passionate Pilgrim* (1599) contains only five authenticated poems (two sonnets and three verses from *Love's Labour's Lost*); *The Phoenix and the Turtle* (1601) may be his, but the authenticity of *A Lover's Complaint* (appended to the first edition of the sonnets) is highly questionable.

Who Was Shakespeare? At this point we might mention a problem that has plagued Shakespeare study for over a century: who was Shakespeare? Those who would like to make the author of the plays someone else—Francis Bacon or the Earl of Oxford or even Christopher Marlowe (dead long before most of the plays were written)—have used the lack of information of Shakespeare's early years and the confusion in the evidence we have been examining to advance their candidate. But the major arguments against Shakespeare show the source of these speculators' disbelief to be in class-conscious snobbery, and perhaps in a perverse adherence to minority opinion. The most common argument is that no one of Shakespeare's background, lack of education, and lack of aristocratic experience could know all that the author knew. But study will reveal that such information was readily available in various popular sources, that some of it lies in the literary sources used for the play, and that Shakespeare was probably not totally lacking in education or in social decorum. The more significant question of style and tone is not dealt with—nor could it successfully be raised. Bacon, for example, no matter how we admire his mind and his writings, exhibits a writing style diametrically opposite to Shakespeare's, a style most unpoetic and often flat. The student would be wise not to waste time rehashing these unfounded theories. No such question was raised in the seventeenth or eighteenth centuries, and no serious student of the plays today doubts that Shakespeare *was* Shakespeare.

COMPLETE BACKGROUND

Shakespeare's England

The world of Elizabethan and Jacobean England was a world of growth and change. The great increase in the middle class, and in the population as a whole, demanded a new economy and means of livelihood, a new instrument of government (one recognizing "rights" and changed class structure), a new social code, and a broad base of entertainment. The invention of printing a century before had contributed to that broader base, but it was the theater that supplied the more immediate needs of the greatest numbers. The theater grew and along with it came less-educated, more money-conscious writers, who gave the people what they wanted: entertainment. But Shakespeare, having passed through a brief period of hack writing, proceeded to set down important ideas in memorable language throughout most of his career. His plays, particularly the later ones, have been analyzed by recent critics in terms of literary quality through their metaphor, verse-line, relationships with psychology and myth, and elaborate structure. Yet Shakespeare was a man of the stage, and the plays were written to be performed. Only this will fully account for the humor of a deadly serious play like *Hamlet* or the spectacle of a *Coriolanus*.

Life in London During Shakespeare's early years there, London was a walled city of about 200,000, with seven gates providing access to the city from the east, north, and west. It was geographically small and crisscrossed by narrow little streets and lanes. The various wards each had a parish church that dominated the life of the close-knit community. To the south and outside the city were slums and the haunts of criminal types; and farther out were the agricultural lands and huge estates. As the population increased and the central area declined, the fashionable people of the city moved toward the west where the palace of Westminster lay. Houses were generally rented out floor by floor and sometimes room by room. Slums were common within the city too, though close to pleasant enough streets and squares. "Merrie Olde England" was not really clean, nor were its people, for in those days there were no sewers or drains except the gutter in the middle of the street, into which garbage would be emptied to be floated off by the rain to Fleet ditch or Moor ditch. Plague was particularly ravaging in 1592, 1593-94 (when the theaters were closed to avoid contamination), and 1603. Medical knowledge, of course, was slight; ills were "cured" by amputation, leeching, blood-letting, and cathartics. The city was (and still is) dominated by St. Paul's Cathedral, around which booksellers clustered on Pasternoster Row.

Religious Atmosphere Of great significance for the times was religion. Under Elizabeth, a state church had developed; it was Protestant in nature and was called Angli-

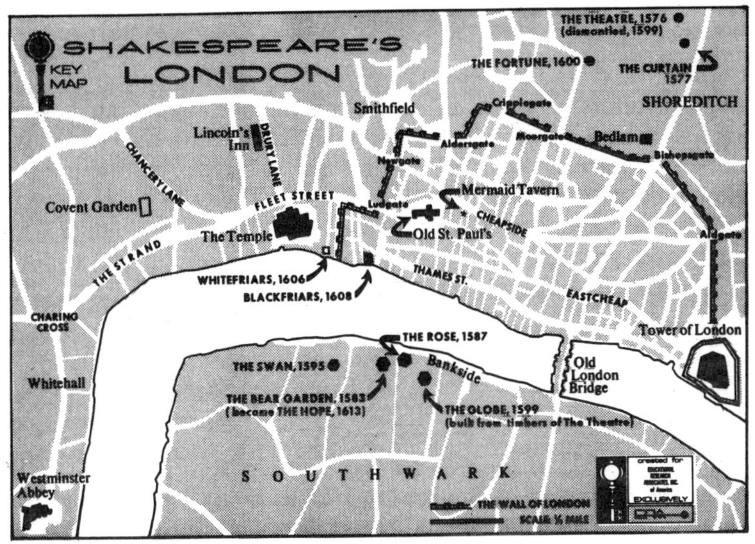

can (or, in America, Episcopalian), but it had arisen from Henry VIII's break with the Pope and from a compromise with the Roman Catholics who had gained power under Mary Tudor.

The Church of England, nominally headed by the reigning monarch, was actually controlled by the Archbishop of Canterbury, who was to be an increasingly important political figure in the early part of the seventeenth century. There were also many schismatic groups, which generally desired further departures from Roman Catholicism. Calvinists were perhaps the most numerous and important of the Protestant groups. The Puritans, who were Calvinist, desired to "purify" the church of ritual and certain dogmas, but during the 1590's they were lampooned as extremist in dress and conduct.

Political Milieu and Contemporary Events During Shakespeare's lifetime there were two monarchs: Elizabeth, 1558-1603, and James I, 1603-1625. Elizabeth was the daughter of Henry VIII and Anne Boleyn, his second wife, who was executed in 1536. After Henry's death his son by his third wife, Jane Seymour (who died in 1537), reigned as Edward VI. He was followed by Mary Tudor, daughter of Henry's first wife, Catherine of Aragon. Mary was a Roman Catholic who tried to put down religious dissension caused by her father's break with Rome on the one hand and her marriage to Philip II of Spain on the other. She persecuted those who wished reunion with the Papacy as well as those whose thought envisioned subservience to Catholic Spain.

Elizabeth's reign was troubled by many overtures of marriage, particularly from Spanish and French nobles—all Roman Catholic—and by the people's concern for an heir to the throne. English suitors generally canceled one another out by intrigue or aggressiveness. One of the most prominent was the Earl of Essex, Robert Devereux, who fell in and out of favor; he apparently attempted to take over the reins of control, only to be captured, imprisoned, and executed in February 1601. One claimant to the throne was Mary of Scotland, a Roman Catholic and widow of Francis II of France. She was the second cousin of Elizabeth, tracing her claim through her grandmother, who was Henry VIII's sister (see KEY CHART, below). Finally settlement came with Elizabeth's acceptance of Mary's son (by her second marriage) as heir apparent, though Mary was to be captured, tried, and executed for treason in 1587. Mary had abdicated the throne of Scotland in 1567 in favor of her son, James VI. His ascent to the throne of England in 1603 as James I joined the two kingdoms for the first time, although Scotland during the seventeenth century often acted independently of England.

Political and religious problems were intermingled in the celebrated Gunpowder Plot. A group of Catholics plotted to blow up Parliament, and James with it, at its first session on November 5, 1605. The plot was discovered before it could be carried out and Guy Fawkes, on duty at the time, was apprehended.

Among the most noteworthy public events during these times were the wars with the Spanish, which included the defeat of the Spanish Armada in 1588, the battle in the Lowlands in

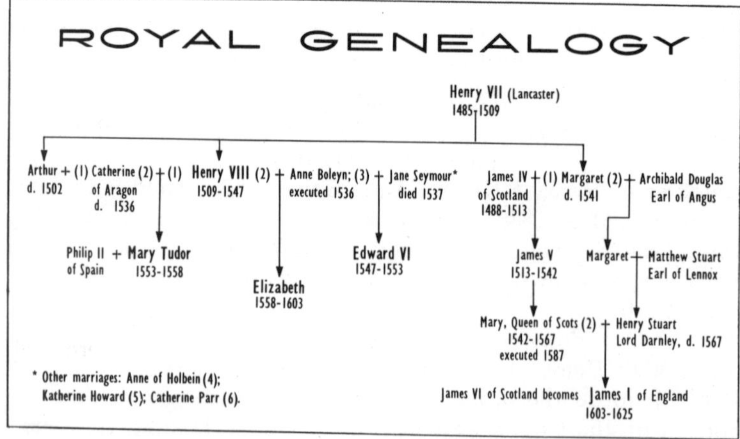

1590-1594, the expedition to Cadiz under Essex in 1596, and the expedition to the Azores (the Islands Expedition) also under Essex in 1597. With trading companies especially set up for colonization and exploitation, travel excited the imagination of the people: here was a new way of life, here were new customs brought back by the sailors and merchants, here was a new dream world to explore.

In all, the years from around 1590 to 1601 were trying ones for English people, relieved only by the news from abroad, the new affluence, and the hope for the future under James. Writers of the period frequently reflect, however, the disillusionment and sadness of those difficult times.

The Elizabethan Theater

Appearance The Elizabethan playhouse developed from the medieval inn with its rooms grouped around a courtyard into which a stage was built. This pattern was used in The Theatre, built by James Burbage in 1576: a square frame building (later round or octagonal) with a square yard, three tiers of galleries, each jutting out over the one below, and a stage extending into the middle of the yard, where people stood or sat on improvised seats. There was no cover over the yard or stage, and lighting was therefore natural. Thus performances were what we might consider late matinees or early evening performances; in summer, daylight continues in London until around ten o'clock.

Other theaters were constructed during the ensuing years: The Curtain in 1577, The Rose in 1587 (on Bankside), The Swan in 1595 (also Bankside), and Shakespeare's playhouse, The Globe, in 1599 (not far from The Rose). There is still some question about the exact dimensions of this house, but it seems to have been octagonal, each side measuring about 36 feet, with an over-all diameter of 84 feet. It was about 33 feet to the eaves, and the yard was 56 feet in diameter. Three sides were used for backstage and to serve the needs of the players. There was no curtain or proscenium; hence the spectators became part of the action. Obviously the actors' asides and soliloquies were effective under these conditions.

There was no real scenery and there were only a few major props; thus the lines of the play had to reveal locations and movement, changes in time or place, etc. In this way, too, it was easier to establish a nonrealistic setting, for all settings were created in words. On either side of the stage were doors, within the flooring were trapdoors (for entrances of ghosts, etc.), and behind the main stage was the inner stage or recess. Here indoor scenes (such as a court or a bedchamber) were played, and some props could be used because the inner stage was usually concealed by a curtain when not in use. It might also have served to hide someone behind the ever-present arras, like Polonius in *Hamlet*. The "chamber" was on the second level, with windows and a balcony. On the third level was another chamber primarily for musicians.

Actors An acting company such as the Lord Chamberlain's Men was a fellowship of ten to fifteen sharers with some ten to twelve extras, three or four boys (often to play women's roles) who might become full sharers, and stagehands. There were rival companies, each with its leading dramatist and leading tragic actor and clown. The Lord Admiral's Men, organized in 1594, boasted Ben Jonson and the tragedian Edward Alleyn. Some of the rivalry of this War of the Theaters is reflected in the speeches of Hamlet, who also comments on the ascendancy and unwarranted popularity of children's companies (like the Children of Blackfriars) in the late 1590's.

The company dramatist, of course, had to think in terms of the members of his company as he wrote his play. He had to make use of the physical features and peculiar talents of the actors, making sure, besides, that there was a role for each member. The fact that women's parts were taken by boys imposed obvious limitations on the range of action. Accordingly, we often find women characters impersonating men; for example, Robert Goffe played Portia in *The Merchant of Venice,* and Portia impersonates a male lawyer in the important trial scene. Goffe also played Juliet, and Anne in *Richard III,* and Oberon in *Midsummer-Night's Dream.* The influence of an actor on the playwright can be seen, on the one hand, by noting the "humor" characters portrayed so competently by Thomas Pope, who was a choleric Mercutio in *Romeo and Juliet,* a melancholic Jaques in *As You Like It,* and a sanguinary Falstaff in *1 Henry IV*, and by comparing, on the other hand, the clown Bottom in *Midsummer-Night's Dream,* played in a frolicsome manner by William Kempe, with the clown Feste in *Twelfth Night,* sung and danced by Robert Armin. Obviously too, if a certain kind of character was not available within the company, then that kind of character could not be written into the play. The approach was decidedly different from ours today, where the play almost always comes first and the casting of roles second. The plays were performed in a repertory system, with a different play each afternoon. The average life of a play was about ten performances.

History of the Drama English drama goes back to native forms developed from playlets presented at Church holidays. Mystery plays dealt with biblical stories such as the Nativity or the Passion, and miracle plays usually depicted the lives of saints. The merchant and craft guilds that came to own and produce the cycles of plays were the forerunners of the theatrical companies of Shakespeare's time. The kind of production these cycles received, either as moving pageants in the streets or as staged shows in a churchyard, influenced the late sixteenth-century production of a secular play: there was an intimacy with the audience, and there was a great reliance on words rather than setting and props. Similar involvement with the stage action is experienced by audiences of the arena theater of today.

The morality play, the next form to develop, was an allegory of the spiritual conflict between good and evil in the soul of man. The *dramatis personae* were abstract virtues and vices, with at least one man representing Mankind (or Everyman, as the most popular of these plays was titled). Some modern critics see *Othello* as a kind of morality play in which the soul of Othello is vied for by the aggressively evil Iago (as a kind of Satanic figure) and the passively good Desdemona (as a personification of Christian faith in all men). The Tudor interlude—a short, witty, visual play—may have influenced the subplot of the Elizabethan play with its low-life and jesting and visual tricks. In mid-sixteenth century appeared the earliest known English comedies, Nicholas Udall's *Ralph Roister Doister* and *Gammer Gurton's Needle* (of uncertain authorship). Both show the influence of the Roman comic playwright Plautus. Shakespeare's *Comedy of Errors,* performed in the 1590's, was an adaptation of Plautus' *Menaechmi,* both plays featuring twins and an involved story of confused identities. The influence of the Roman tragedian Seneca can be traced from Thomas Norton and Thomas Sackville in *Gorboduc* to *Hamlet.* Senecan tragedy is a tragedy of revenge, characterized by many deaths, much blood-letting, ghosts, feigned madness, and the motif of a death for a death.

Shakespeare's Artistry

Plots Generally a Shakespearean play has two plots: a main plot and a subplot. The subplot reflects the main plot and is often concerned with inferior characters. Two contrasting examples will suffice: Lear and his daughters furnish the characters for the main plot of filial love and ingratitude, whereas Gloucester and his sons enact the same theme in the subplot; Lear and Gloucester both learn that outward signs of love may be false. In *Midsummer-Night's Dream* the town workmen (Quince, Bottom, *et al.*) put on a tragic play in such a hilarious way that it turns the subject of the play—love so strong that the hero will kill himself if his loved one dies first—into farce; but this in the main plot is the "serious" plight of the four mixed-up lovers. In both examples Shakespeare has reinforced his points by subplots dealing with the same subject as the main plot.

Sources The plots of the Elizabethan plays were usually adapted from other sources. "Originality" was not the sought quality; a kind of variation on a theme was. It was felt that one could better evaluate the playwright's worth by seeing what he did with a familiar tale. What he stressed, how he stressed it, how he restructured the familiar elements—these were the important matters. Shakespeare closely followed Sir Thomas North's very popular translation of Plutarch's Life of Marcus Antonius, for example, in writing *Antony and Cleopatra;* and he modified Robert Greene's *Pandosto* and combined it with the Pygmalion myth in *The Winter's Tale,* while drawing the character of Autolycus from certain pamphlets written by Greene. The only plays for which sources have not been clearly determined are *Love's Labour's Lost* (probably based on contemporary events) and *The Tempest* (possibly based on some shipwreck account from travelers to the New World).

Verse and Prose There is a mixture of verse and prose in the plays, partially because plays fully in verse were out of fashion. Greater variety could thus be achieved, and character or atmosphere could be more precisely delineated. Elevated passages, philosophically significant ideas, speeches by men of high rank are in verse; but comic and light parts, speeches including dialect or broken English, and scenes that move more rapidly or simply give mundane information are in prose. The poetry is almost always blank verse (iambic pentameter lines without rhyme). Rhyme is used, however (particularly the couplet), to mark the close of scenes or an important action. Rhyme also serves as a cue for the entrance of another actor or some off-stage business, to point to a change of mood or thought, as a forceful opening after a passage of prose, to convey excitement or passion or sentimentality, and to distinguish characters.

Shakespeare's plays may be divided into three general categories, though some plays are not readily classified and further subdivisions may be suggested within a category.

The History Play The history play, or chronicle, may tend to tragedy, like *Richard II,* or to comedy, like *1 Henry IV.* It is a chronicle of some royal personage, often altered for dramatic purposes, even to the point of falsification of the facts. Its popularity may have resulted from the rising nationalism of the English, nurtured by their successes against the Spanish, their developing trade and colonization, and their rising prestige as a world power. The chronicle was considered a political guide, like the popular *Mirror for Magistrates,* a collection of writings showing what happens when an important leader falls through some error in his ways, his thinking, or his personality. Thus the history play counseled the right path by negative, if not positive, means. Accordingly, it is difficult to call *Richard II* a tragedy, since Richard was wrong and his wrongness harmed his people. The political philosophy of Shakespeare's day seemed to favor the view that all usurpation was bad and should be corrected, but not by further usurpation. When that original usurpation had been established, through an heir's ascension to the throne, it was to be accepted. Then any rebellion against the "true" king would be a rebellion against God.

Tragedy Tragedy in simple terms meant that the protagonist died. Certain concepts drawn from Aristotle's *Poetics* require a tragic hero of high standing, who must oppose some conflicting force, either external or internal. The tragic hero should be dominated by a *hamartia* (a so-called tragic flaw, but really an *excess* of some character trait, e.g., pride, or *hubris*), and it is this *hamartia* that leads to his downfall and, because of his status, to the downfall of others. The action presented in the tragedy must be recognizable to the audience as real and potential; through seeing it enacted, the audience has its passion (primarily suffering) raised, and the conclusion of the action thus brings release from that passion (*catharsis*). However, a more meaningful way of looking at tragedy in the Elizabethan theater is to see it as that which occurs when essential good (like Hamlet) is wasted (through disaster or death) in the process of driving out evil (such as Claudius represents).

Comedy Comedy in simple terms meant that the play ended happily for the protagonists. Sometimes the comedy depends on exaggerations of man's eccentricities—comedy of humours; sometimes the comedy is romantic and far-fetched. The romantic comedy was usually based on a mix-up in events or confused identity of characters, particularly by disguise. It moved toward tragedy in that an important person might die and the mix-up might never be unraveled; but in the nick of time something happened or someone appeared (sometimes illogically or unexpectedly) and saved the day. It reflects the structure of myth by moving from happiness to despair to resurrection. *The Winter's Tale* is a perfect example of this, for the happiness of the first part is banished with Hermione's exile and Perdita's abandonment; tragedy is near when the lost baby, Perdita, cannot be found and Hermione is presumed dead; but Perdita reappears as does Hermione, a statue that suddenly comes to life. Lost identities are established and confusions disappear; but the mythic-comic nature of the play is seen in the reuniting of the mother, Hermione, a kind of Ceres, with her daughter, Perdita, a kind of Proserpina. Spring returns, summer will bring the harvest, and the winter of the tale is left behind—for a little while.

What is it, then, that makes Shakespeare's art so great? Perhaps we see in it a whole spectrum of humanity, treated impersonally, but with kindness and understanding. We seldom meet in Shakespeare a weeping philosopher: he may criticize, but he criticizes both sides. After he has done so, he gives the impression of saying, Well, that's the way life is; people will always be like that—don't get upset about it. This is probably the key to the Duke's behavior in *Measure for Measure*—a most unbitter comedy despite former labels. Only in *Hamlet* does Shakespeare not seem to fit this statement; it is the one play that Shakespeare the person enters.

As we grow older and our range of experience widens, so too does Shakespeare's range seem to expand. Perhaps this lies in the ambiguities of his materials, which allow for numerous individual readings. We meet our own experiences—and they are ours alone, we think—expressed in phrases that we thought our own or of our own discovery. What makes Shakespeare's art so great, then, is his ability to say so much to so many people in such memorable language: he is himself "the show and gaze o' the time."

Introduction to the Play

Sources During the Renaissance there was much less emphasis put on a writer's originality than there is today. What commanded esteem was the writer's artistic use of his material, not the fact that it was his own. This was particularly true in the drama. In this, as in a number of other respects, Elizabethan drama resembled our own "movies," which are so heavily dependent on novels and plays for their material.

The dramas of Shakespeare are no exception, as we have seen on p. 22. Scholars have found sources for almost every one of them. The study of these sources has been one of the main areas of Shakespearean scholarship. Not only is finding the works to which Shakespeare is indebted interesting in itself, but by observing what he took from these works, what he left out, and what he changed we can see his craftsmanship at work, cast light upon some obscurities, and be guided to his artistic intentions.

The major and perhaps only source of *Macbeth* is Raphael Holinshed's *Chronicles of England, Scotlande and Irelande* (1577), which was also a major source for Shakespeare's English history plays and a source for portions of *King Lear* and *Cymbeline*. Scholars have argued for other works as additional sources for *Macbeth,* but it is often hard to say whether or not a supposed parallel is merely a coincidence and a supposed verbal echo is merely a use of a commonplace of the time. At all events, it is clear that Shakespeare's chief indebtedness is to Holinshed's history.

Here Shakespeare found most of the detail for his tragedy. The most significant changes that he made were as follows: many of the facts in the murder of Shakespeare's Duncan come not from Holinshed's account of that murder but from his account of the murder of another king, Duff, by the nobleman Donwald and his wife; Macbeth's character is blackened; Banquo, on the other hand, is cleared of guilt. What Shakespeare evidently sought to do was to make Macbeth's crime as heinous as possible. Therefore, instead of using the facts of the killing of Duncan, an assassination that was done in the open, he uses those of the murder done by Donwald, who was the host of Duff, drugged his grooms, and put on a display of innocence and indignation. Donwald had the aid, however, of four servants, and this Shakespeare omitted in order to focus on Macbeth and fasten full responsibility on him. Furthermore, in Holinshed Macbeth had reason to feel aggrieved against Duncan, and Duncan was not an old, saintly king but a young, feeble one.

What Shakespeare therefore did was, with the audacity of genius, to make it as difficult as possible for himself to gain the audience's sympathy for Macbeth. Yet he succeeded magnificently in doing so by causing the audience to appreciate the intensity of his temptation, to perceive the power of evil, and above all to share his terrors. Banquo, who was supposed to be the ancestor of Shakespeare's own King James, Shakespeare makes a foil for Macbeth. In Holinshed he was one of Macbeth's accomplices in the assassination of Duncan, but Shakespeare makes him resist evil in contrast with Macbeth, who succumbs to it.

Scottish Historical Background During the tenth century the united kingdoms of Scotland, known as Alban, comprised the land north of the Firths of Forth and Clyde (see KEY MAP, p. 5). Malcolm II (1005-34) and his grandson Duncan I (1034-40) added the lands south to Solway Firth and the Tweed River. Attempted invasion by the Norsemen, who had acquired footholds in the various islands surrounding Scotland, was repulsed during Duncan's reign. Macbeth, the steward (*mormaor*) of Ross and Moray, ended much of the internal strife in 1040 when he assassinated the king and assumed the throne. In 1057 he was defeated by Duncan's son, who ascended the throne as Malcolm III, ruling until his death in 1093. His reign was significant for its transformation of Celtic culture into English culture and the influence of Roman Catholicism through Malcolm's English wife Margaret.

The world of *Macbeth* is a world of an early feudalism which has barely managed to establish a precarious social order. This world in the rocky highlands of Scotland is hard and primitive, abounding in violence. But in this world Macbeth is a heroic figure (at first), a valiant warrior loyally serving his king. He disdains the fortune of battle that seemed to smile upon the rebel and wins despite it by his heroic deeds. Such valor is rewarded by the king by title and land, and the crown itself was not at this time hereditary. A council of nobles would elect a new king from among the members of the royal family after the death of the previous king. However, a successor was frequently declared in the lifetime of the reigning king, and in such an event the title of Prince of Cumberland was given to him. The formal conferral of the title upon Malcolm would have meant that the nobility had recognized him as heir-apparent.

From Holinshed Shakespeare got a picture of a primitive feudalism still attempting to impose social order, of violent acts, black treachery, and oppressive remorse. This cultural setting contributes to the distinctive atmosphere of *Macbeth*, with its gloomy castles able to "laugh a siege to scorn," its boding ravens, heavily barred gates, alarum bells that call to arms, barren heaths, and savage hand-to-hand conflicts.

However, while removing the tragedies from the here and now, Shakespeare generally made use of references to the things of his day. These were once decried as anachronisms that were the result of either his ignorance or his carelessness, but they are now seen as artistic means by which Shakespeare made the events of the past have relevance to the present and made the events of the present have a universal significance. In this, *Macbeth* is like Shakespeare's other tragedies.

Topicality The Scottish setting of *Macbeth* gave it an immediate topical appeal. The date of its first performance has generally been placed by scholars in 1606. In 1603 James VI of Scotland ascended to the throne and became James I of England. There had been a great deal of anxiety concerning who was to be the successor to Elizabeth, and when James became king without bloodshed there was general relief. The prophecy that Banquo's descendants would not only hold the kingdom of Scotland but would join it with that of England in a union that would be ruled by his line into the indefinite future would therefore have accorded with the atmosphere of the time.

The presence of the witches in *Macbeth*, although they are derived from Holinshed, also has a special topical significance, for James was convinced that he was the victim of witchcraft. His mortal enemy, his cousin the younger Bothwell, was convicted of seeking to cause his death through witchcraft. James also attributed to witchcraft the great storms that repeatedly drove back the ship bringing his bride from Denmark. He himself interrogated old women charged with being witches and elicited from them confessions to having performed such impossibilities as going to sea in sieves such as the witches speak of in *Macbeth.*

Most important of all the topical references, however, is that of the Porter to the equivocator who committed treason in God's name but could not equivocate his way to heaven. This alludes to Father Garnet, who in the Gunpowder Plot trial was charged with having made use of the Jesuit doctrine of equivocation that permitted one to swear under duress something to which he made internal mental reservations. The Gunpowder Plot, which sought to destroy at one blow king and parliament, made a terrific impact on the popular imagination, so much so that its discovery is still celebrated in England as Guy Fawkes Day. The Scottish Privy Council proclaimed that it was diabolically inspired. James compared it in its heinousness to the sensational murder of his father, between which and the murder of Duff, used by Shakespeare in his representation of the murder of Duncan, contemporary historians drew parallels. In short, the violence permeating *Macbeth* is not merely the violence of primitive Scotland; it is also the violence of Renaissance Scotland and Renaissance England, and it would have been perceived as such. This perception would have brought home to Shakespeare's audience that the struggle between good and evil is an everlasting one.

By using our historical imaginations, we can appreciate how the charged atmosphere of Shakespeare's time affected the audience's response to *Macbeth.* Such an appreciation can heighten its meaningfulness for us. The perception of how Shakespeare universalized the contemporary may indeed suggest parallels with our own day, such as a comparison between Macbeth and a dictator like Stalin, who like Macbeth betrayed his own early principles, became paranoic and suspicious of everyone as a threat to his power, indulged in blood purges, kept an army of spies and secret agents, and killed members of the families of those who had defected or been exiled. The knowledge of the Elizabethan Shakespeare makes him come alive in the twentieth century.

The Witches Witches were not a Hallowe'en joke in Shakespeare's day. They and other manifestations of the supernatural were widely believed in, probably by almost everyone, educated as well as uneducated. The beginnings of modern rationalism were at work, for Reginald Scot wrote a book attacking belief in witches, but the shocked response of

James I, who ordered the book burned and wrote one of his own in reply, was doubtless typical.

Shakespeare gave his "weird sisters" the customary features of witches of his day. They have animals—a cat, a toad—who are really "familiars," evil spirits who have taken this bodily form. They arrange to meet in a thunderstorm, as if they can affect the weather, as they were supposed to be able to do. There is frequent reference to the owl, a customary "familiar" of witches. Macbeth has bad dreams, and these were notoriously caused by witches, as were such hallucinations as the "air-drawn dagger." Indeed the very word "nightmare," often also called in Shakespeare's time "night hag" or "the riding of the witch," refers to a witch riding wildly through the night on horseback, visiting bad dreams on her victims.

What, however, are the limits of the powers of the witches and from where do they derive these powers? On these points there was confusion in popular and learned belief. Witches could be regarded as old women who were given supernatural powers by the devil, to whom they had sold their souls, or as demons who had assumed the bodies of old women for their evil purposes. They were also identified with the classical furies, who were goddesses of punishment, and with fairies and elves, creatures of folklore who were more sinister than we think of them today. Some writers called witches "weirds" (derived from an old English word meaning "fate"), and Holinshed, in giving one explanation of the three women who met Macbeth (another is that they are "nymphs or fairies, endued with knowledge of prophecy") used "weird sisters" to refer to "the goddesses of destiny," the Parcae of classical mythology or the Norns of Scandinavian mythology.

Shakespeare's witches are a compound of native folklore and classical mythology. They are called the weird sisters throughout the play except by the sailor's wife and in the stage-directions, where they are referred to as witches. They serve demons, for they are summoned by their "familiars" and conjure up apparitions whom they call masters. Their use of cauldrons for divination is borrowed from the practice of classical furies, not from that of native witches. They are associated with Hecate, the Greek goddess of sorcery and the other world, who is referred to in portions of the play other than the non-Shakespearean interpolations in which she appears.

Although the witches can foretell the future, the general

tenor of the play suggests that Macbeth bears responsibility for his own actions, that they can strongly tempt and influence him but are not in control of his destiny. There is, to be sure, an air of fatalism in the predestined role of Macduff, but fundamentally Macbeth brings his own doom upon himself in being driven by the torments of his own sense of guilt into a fearful insecurity that causes him to commit further guilty crimes. His crucial decision to kill Lady Macduff and her children is his own, although the witches could foresee that, once having attempted to escape the consequences of his guilt through further crime, he would land in that final trap.

The sharpest expression of the free will of the two central characters is Lady Macbeth's invocation of evil spirits. She deliberately chooses evil as her good. Elizabethans would have regarded her as literally possessed by the spirits she has summoned. Similarly, Macbeth chooses to murder Duncan and does not blame the witches for having made this choice. He only blames them later for having deceived him with false promises. He is tempted by the forces of evil and driven to despair by them when he succumbs, losing his soul, but his soul is his own to keep or lose.

We no longer believe in witches, but we can give dramatic credence to them, for if we do not believe in "the riding of the witch," we still have nightmares. Moreover, in giving dramatic credence to them, we can recognize them and the devil they serve as symbolic of the evil to which men succumb. Paraphrasing an ancient question, we may say, "What does it profit a man to gain the kingdom of Scotland and lose his own personal integrity?" As long as men do evil to others and betray their own principles, as long as there is war and injustice, the witches' hell-brew still bubbles.

A Note on the Text The only authoritative text of *Macbeth* is that of the First Folio (1623). It is apparently an acting version, abridged and changed from its original form and augmented by scenes or songs written by Thomas Middleton. Abridgment is suggested by the lack of a substantial subplot and by the fact that this is the shortest of Shakespeare's tragedies. Alterations are evidenced by prosodic and punctuational problems. However, the substantive text does not seem to be corrupt. Middleton's additions, taken from his play *The Witch* (ca. 1612), are the scenes involving Hecate and the witches' songs: III,v; IV,i,38-43, 125-132.

Stage History

The first reference to *Macbeth* is a note by the astrologer Dr. Simon Forman that he saw it enacted at the Globe on April 20, 1611. Richard Burbage (1567?-1619), "the English Roscius," created the title role. The Restoration saw a revision of the tragedy into a kind of opera with flying witches and dancing, by Sir William Davenant, who had received a royal warrant for various Shakespearean plays at the end of 1660. John Downes tells us in *Roscius Anglicanus* (1708) that the Duke's Theatre (Dorset Garden) production in 1673 "recompensed double the expense" of all the new finery and scenery and machines. At times the text was "reformed" to remove Shakespeare's indecorousness and obscurity: for example, the "cream-fac'd loon" becomes a "Friend," and a "goose look" becomes a "change of countenance." The leading actor of the Duke's Company, Thomas Betterton (1635?-1710), played Macbeth, and first his wife, Mrs. Saunderson (?-1711), and then Elizabeth Barry (1658-1713) undertook Lady Macbeth. This version held the stage until 1744 with such men as Robert Wilks (1665?-1732) in the lead.

David Garrick revised the play to restore much of its tragic qualities in the Drury Lane presentation of 1743 except that he added a rather sentimental dying speech for Macbeth in which he lamented his fate. Hannah Pritchard (1711-1768) was the most renowned interpreter of Lady Macbeth during this time; she acted in Garrick's company. In 1773 Charles Macklin (1697?-1797) gave his audience actors in kilts against a setting placed in the Highlands. John Philip Kemble (1757-1823), a fine Macbeth, returned to the singing and dancing witches of Davenant's version while retaining Garrick's speech for the dying hero. He was joined by his sister, the fabled Sarah Siddons (1775-1831), as Lady Macbeth in this Drury Lane production of 1794. Later his witches became more truly evil spirits writhing in blackness.

The nineteenth century saw such significant performances of the play as William Charles Macready's (1793-1873) in a fuller restoring of Shakespeare's text; Samuel Phelps' (1804-1878) in 1847; Henry Irving's (1838-1905) in 1888; and Johnston Forbes-Robertson's (1853-1937) in 1898. The lavish production of Herbert Beerbohm Tree (1853-1917) in 1911 was not yet really twentieth-century in style. The opera by Verdi with a libretto fairly close to Shakespeare has been revived most successfully in recent years. The play has been popular as a vehicle for major actors and, of course, with all the Festival groups. Part of its popularity with the general public, however, stems from its being standard school reading. Notable renditions have been those of Lyn Harding and Florence Reed in 1928; of Maurice Evans and Judith Anderson in 1941; and of Michael Redgrave and Flora Robson in 1948. Orson Welles put the play on film in 1948; and television has frequently offered an abbreviated version with Evans and Anderson.

CAPSULE SUMMARY

Act I Macbeth has subdued first a rebellion and then an invasion of Scotland by Norwegian troops assisted by a traitor, the Thane of Cawdor. Accompanied by his fellow commander Banquo, he meets three witches on his way back from battle. They greet him as the Thane of Glamis, as the Thane of Cawdor, and as the future king. When he starts back affrighted, Banquo asks the witches what the future holds in store for him. They inform him that he will found a line of kings although he himself will not be king. Macbeth challenges them, pointing out that he does not have the title of Thane of Cawdor, but when two noblemen arrive with the message that the king has divested the traitor of this title to confer it upon him, Macbeth is shaken by the verification of the witches' words and by the horrible thought of murder which comes to him.

Macbeth is graciously received by King Duncan, who as a mark of his favor announces that he will visit Macbeth in his castle. At the castle, Lady Macbeth, informed of the witches' prophecy by a letter from her husband, expresses fear that Macbeth will not have the ruthlessness to do what is necessary to become king. When Macbeth after his arrival expresses reluctance to commit murder, she urges him on and prevails.

Act II Macbeth, summoning up all his will power, goes to kill the sleeping Duncan. Lady Macbeth waits tensely for his return. When he comes back, it is with blood on his hands and horror in his soul. She urges him to wash the blood off and goes to lay the bloody daggers by the side of the sleeping grooms in order that the suspicion of the murder fall on them.

Macduff, a nobleman appointed to wake Duncan, enters his bed-chamber and rouses the occupants of the castle with his cries. Macbeth rushes to the chamber and kills the grooms, pretending to be carried away by anger. Malcolm and Donalbain, the king's sons, suspicious and fearful, decide to run away, Malcolm to England and Donalbain to Ireland. By doing so, they themselves incur suspicion. Macbeth is chosen king by the council of noblemen and proceeds to the coronation.

Act III Macbeth, now king, has a banquet to which he invites Banquo, whom he fears. Macbeth is also tormented by his recollection of the prophecy that Banquo will be the father of kings, a prophecy which implies that he himself will not found a dynasty. He plans to have Banquo and his young son Fleance murdered on their way to the banquet, but Fleance runs away as the assassins fall upon his father. At the banquet Macbeth is dismayed when, on his expressing his regret at the absence of Banquo, the ghost of Banquo, seen only by himself, appears. He speaks wildly to it, amazing everyone. Lady Macbeth attempts to reassure the company, saying that Macbeth has been subject to such seizures since his youth. Finally, however, the company has to be asked to leave. The nobility now suspects Macbeth, and we are told that Macduff has gone to join Malcolm in England.

Act IV Macbeth, resolved to know what the future has in store for him, goes to see the witches again. They summon apparitions who tell him that he should beware of Macduff, that no man born of woman will harm him, and that he will not be vanquished until Birnam Wood comes to Dunsinane Hill. When he asks them, however, whether Banquo's issue will ever reign in Scotland, they show him a procession of kings, which the ghost of Banquo points to as his. Infuriated by the sight, Macbeth, on being told immediately thereafter that Macduff has fled to England, has Lady Macduff and her young son killed.

In England, Macduff has sought out Malcolm to tell him how Macbeth is bringing new sorrows to his country every day and to urge him to levy an army against the tyrant. Malcolm, to make sure that Macduff is not an agent of Macbeth, accuses himself of sins which make him unfit to rule. When Macduff turns away in despair, Malcolm informs him that he spoke only to test him and that he is preparing to lead an expedition against Macbeth. At this moment the nobleman

Ross comes to tell Macduff of the murder of his wife and children. At first, Macduff is overcome by grief, but he resolves to kill Macbeth when he meets him on the field of battle.

Act V Lady Macbeth, like Macbeth, has been suffering inner torments, and we see her walking in her sleep, reenacting the murder of Duncan and seeking in vain to wash the blood off her hands. As Macbeth, frantic, is preparing to be besieged in his castle at Dunsinane, he is told that his wife has committed suicide, but life is now a meaningless thing for him, and he spends no time lamenting.

In the meantime, Malcolm has ordered that each of his men cut off a bough from Birnam Wood and bear it before him as they advance so that it will be difficult for enemy scouts to determine the size of the army. A soldier who has been standing guard on top of the hill runs to Macbeth to tell him that he saw Birnam Wood moving. Macbeth, who has been relying on the supposed assurance of the witches, orders his men in the frenzy of his despair to leave the castle and attack: at least they will die in battle.

Attacking with the desperate courage of a trapped animal, Macbeth now relies on the assurance that no man born of woman can hurt him. Although his men readily surrender, he continues to fight, determined to continue killing rather than to commit suicide. The sight of Macduff, however, takes him aback, for his soul is burdened by the slaying of Lady Macduff and her children. Macbeth fights, nevertheless, when Macduff attacks him, telling Macduff that his efforts are in vain, for he is fighting against one who cannot be hurt by a man born of woman. When Macduff replies that he was "from his mother's womb/Untimely ripped," Macbeth is momentarily cowed, but he will not yield and dies fighting.

COMPREHENSIVE SUMMARY

Act I

Scene i Amid thunder and lightning three witches make a rendezvous for the purpose of encountering Macbeth after a battle now raging has been concluded. The place of this scene is not specified: we may imagine any desolate spot, as "wither'd" and "wild" as the witches' attire. They agree to meet again on the heath, an open region devoid of vegetation that is apparently a different place from this one.

COMMENTARY: The keynote of the play is struck with the appearance of the three witches. "Hurlyburly" signifies tumult and confusion, that of battle as well as the murder of Duncan, a violation of natural law bringing unnatural confusion and disorder. This slighting term also suggests the contemptuous regard the witches have for the affairs of men. So does "When the battle's lost and won" (4). Every battle is lost by one side and won by the other, but the witches are indifferent as to which it is that does the losing and the winning. The words also have another meaning: Macbeth will win the battle, but he will lose at this time of triumph another, more important battle—that for his soul.

"Fair is foul, and foul is fair" (11) indicates that everything is unnaturally reversed in the world of evil and that everything is ambiguous and uncertain. Nothing is what it seems to be. The unnatural reversal is seen in the fact that the witches are summoned by Graymalkin (a cat), Paddock (a toad) and an unnamed third creature, animals inhabited by evil spirits. These "pets" call them; the pets, as would be normal, are not called by their mistresses. "Fog and filthy air" (12) depicts an atmosphere of confusion in which deceitful evil operates. Wherever the witches meet, however, will be the barrenness of chaos, for evil is sterile and opposed to the plenteousness of nature.

Scene ii King Duncan is told by a captain who has just come from the battle how it proceeded. For a time the issue seemed doubtful. Then the rebel Macdonwald seemed to be winning, but Macbeth made his way to him in battle and slew him. Next, the Norwegian invader made a fresh assault. At this point the strength of the captain, weakened by his wounds, gives out, and he is helped away. The Thane of Ross comes with the latest news of the battle. Again, it seemed as if the Norwegian forces, outnumbering the Scotch, were on the verge of winning, but Macbeth finally carried the day. Duncan announces that the Thane of Cawdor, a traitor who secretly assisted Norway, will be executed and sends Ross to tell Macbeth that the title of the Thane of Cawdor is now his.

COMMENTARY: *Lines 1-44* The first scene, with its thunder and lightning and the startling appearance of the witches, is designed to attract the audience's attention. Having done so, Shakespeare proceeds to his task of exposition. (See "exposition," GLOSSARY-INDEX.)

The captain's account of the battle is full of images of blood, one of the pervading images in the poetry as well as literally on the stage. (See "image," GLOSSARY-INDEX.) The captain himself is a "bloody man" (1), whose "gashes" (42) cause him almost to faint at the end of his speech. Macbeth's sword "smok'd" with "bloody execution" (18); that is, it steamed with the hot blood which it had caused to gush. To reach Macdonwald, Macbeth sliced his way through the men in the front lines (19) as if he were a butcher carving meat. He "unseam'd" Macdonwald "from the nave to th' chops" (22), and Macbeth and Banquo, fighting savagely against the Norwegians, seemed to intend to bathe in the hot blood spouting forth (39). In this world of violence Macbeth is a heroic figure.

If Fortune appeared to be the "whore" (15) of the rebel Macdonwald—Fortune (or, as we sometimes say now, Lady Luck) was personified in Shakespeare's time as a woman whose fickleness often caused her to be called a harlot—Macbeth was "Bellona's bridegroom" (54), married in his martial splendor to the goddess of war. However, he, who here disdains fortune, becomes preoccupied with what is in store for him in the future when evil makes use of his ambition. He, who "fix'd" the rebel Macdonwald's "head upon our battlements" (23), will at the end have his own head held up for display.

Lines 45-67 The last words of the scene, referring to the transfer of Cawdor's title to Macbeth, recall the witches' "When the battle's lost and won." The battle, which had seemed so uncertain, had finally been won by Macbeth. With it he has won a new title—but it was the title of a traitor, and he himself will shortly be false to the king. He defeats two external threats to the kingdom of Scotland but will succumb to the third threat, that within himself.

Scene iii The three witches appear on the heath in the midst of thunder. Waiting for Macbeth, they tell each other of their misdeeds. The first witch, out of vengeance against a sailor's wife, who would not give her the chestnuts she asked for, had given the sailor contrary winds so that he could not make port but sailed for eighty-one weeks without sleep. Macbeth and Banquo enter. Banquo, amazed at the uncanny appearance of the witches, addresses them. They hail Macbeth as the Thane of Glamis and Cawdor who will be king and hail Banquo as one who is lesser than Macbeth and yet greater, less fortunate and yet more fortunate. When Macbeth asks the witches how can he be Thane of Cawdor, since the holder of that title still lives, and it is therefore as unbelievable that he is Cawdor as it is that he will be king, the witches vanish. At this moment Ross enters to announce the new title that Duncan has given Macbeth. Macbeth is thunderstruck, and horrible imaginings come to his mind. Banquo reacts to this news with "What! can the Devil speak true?" (107), but answers himself soon afterwards, with words that Macbeth would have done well to heed, "Oftentimes, to win us to our harm, The instruments of Darkness tell us truths" (123-24). He disregards Banquo's words and accepts the prophecy as an invitation to evil, such as the "horrid image" of himself murdering Duncan, which causes his hair to stand on end and his heart to pound unnaturally. The image is so overwhelming that his powers of action are made incapable of functioning in his contemplation of what seems to be the future. Recalled to himself, Macbeth excuses his abstractedness by saying that he was trying to recall something which had slipped from his mind.

COMMENTARY: *Lines 1-37* Modern audiences often find it difficult to respond to the witches and are inclined to laugh at them in amusement. They are intended indeed to be grotesque but also to be foully redolent of evil, and yet if their spite is petty, they have the power to cause the ship of a sailor whose wife offended them to be tempest-tossed for "weary sev'n-nights nine times nine" (22). The cursed sailor is unable to sleep during this time, as Macbeth will later be unable to sleep. There is, however, a suggestion that their powers are limited: the sailor's ship "cannot be lost" (24). Since life was often compared to a voyage, the powers of evil can cause life's voyage to have a rough ocean, but their malevolence cannot cause a good man to lose his soul.

Having sold themselves to the devil, they play a role in God's scheme of things, testing men by tempting them to evil, but they cannot control the future, which is ruled by divine providence.

Lines 38-88 Macbeth's words as he and Banquo enter—"So foul and fair a day I have not seen" (38)—have several possible meanings. The sentence is purposefully ambiguous. Macbeth may simply be commenting on the changeableness of the weather, which has suddenly become foggy in the presence of the as yet unseen witches; or he may be saying that he has never seen a battle whose outcome was so uncertain, first appearing to be unhappy or foul and then appearing to be happy or fair; or he may be saying that the fair victory and the foul weather are in sharp contrast. Each of these meanings relates to the uncertainty of things. There is, moreover, a further meaning of which he is unaware: his words echo the witches' "Fair is foul, and foul is fair," suggesting that the witches, unknown to Macbeth, have already established a connection between them. Ironically, he does not know how foul a day this will prove to be for him. (See "irony, dramatic," GLOSSARY-INDEX.)

The theme of the difficulty of distinguishing between what is appearance and what is reality is played upon throughout this drama concerned with the evil which, though hidden, is always lurking in wait for us. (See "theme," GLOSSARY-INDEX.) It is specifically raised in Banquo's questioning of the witches. Questions suggest the confusion, uncertainty, and mystery which pervades the play.

The difference between Macbeth and Banquo is noteworthy. When the witches prophesy that Macbeth shall be king, he starts as if in fear. The suggestion is that they give utterance to his own secret thought. When they vanish instead of answering him, he exclaims (82), "Would they had stay'd!" Banquo, however, is surprised by Macbeth's response to what seems "so fair" (52), not knowing that fair words have provoked foul thoughts. The witches knew that Macbeth was ready to be tempted, and his guilty start and absorption in their words testify to that readiness. Banquo, however, true to his words, is not carried away by the witches' prophecy to him, secure as he is in the staunchness of his soul.

Lines 89-156 When Macbeth hears himself hailed by Ross as the Thane of Cawdor, he replies with an image of himself as dressed in the garments of another man (108-9), a recurrent image, as in ll. 144-146 of this scene.

It is a picture of Macbeth as a usurper: the kingship which he will take does not belong to him.

The bodily effect of the image which the prophecy of his kingship raises in him rests upon a tenet of contemporary logic; that is, correspondence. The Elizabethans believed the human body to be a microcosm, a little world analogous to the universe, and analogous also to the "body politic," human society, which is organized on the same principle of natural order as the body and the universe. Violation of the natural order of society by the killing of a king was thought to result in disorder in the other two spheres, and throughout the play it is suggested, as here, that Macbeth's own body is in unnatural rebellion against him. The very idea of murder "shakes" his "single state of man" (140), his mind and body, which should be, like the political state, an integrated unity.

In the battle, we have been told, Macbeth was "nothing afeard" of what he himself made. The actual corpses which he created seemed unreal in their dreadfulness. He was undismayed by these, too intent on inflicting death to be afraid of it. The corpse which he sees only in his imagination, however, seems overpoweringly real and causes him to tremble violently. But then, the killings on the battle-field were performed in accordance with his duty as a soldier fighting for his king; the murder he sees in his imagination is a murder of the king in violation of his duty. Proceeding, Macbeth finds only his imagination real (142), another aspect of the theme of the difference between appearance and reality. And it is only through his powerful imagination that his conscience works. At various times in the play, as here, he seems to be living in a hideous dream. The reason he offers for his distractedness is a lie, but in one sense what he says may be true: his mind has been seeking to subdue previously repressed thoughts which the witches' prophecy had caused to re-emerge into his consciousness.

Scene iv In the palace at Forres, Duncan is informed of the execution of the former Thane of Cawdor. He comments that one cannot tell the disposition of a man's mind from his face and that he had absolute trust in Cawdor. As he is in the midde of his sentence, Macbeth enters and is greeted with effusive thanks by Duncan. Duncan announces that he will make Malcolm heir to the throne. Macbeth in an aside states that this announcement is a bar to his ambition and calls upon darkness to cover what he wishes to be done. He goes on to call upon his eyes to wink upon what his hand does so that when they open again that which they fear to see will have been done. The King as a mark of his favor proposes to visit Macbeth's castle at Inverness, and Macbeth rides on ahead to prepare a hospitable reception for him.

COMMENTARY: *Lines 1-47* The scene shows how ironically Duncan is deceived in Macbeth, as he had been in the previous Thane of Cawdor. History repeats itself because evil, although masked, is an abiding reality in human nature. Duncan is a gracious old king, overflowing with kindliness. His use of imagery of planting and tilling (28-29) is indicative of his bounteousness and suggests, moreover, the naturalness of the relationship between the king and his subjects. "I have begun to plant thee" refers to his recent conferral on Macbeth of the title of Thane of Cawdor. The familiar "thou" instead of the more formal "you" indicates Duncan's affection towards his relative, who is the savior of his kingdom. If Macbeth had not destroyed himself by murdering Duncan to gain the kingship, he would have continued to grow in honor, the true honor which comes from the public recognition of good deeds, for Duncan would have labored to make him "full of growing."

Before Duncan's announcement that Malcolm will be declared Prince of Cumberland, Macbeth might well have had reason to hope that he, rather than the young and inexperienced Malcolm, would have been chosen by the electors. In his joy over Macbeth's victories, therefore, Duncan is unwittingly bringing his own death upon himself—this despite the fact that Macbeth would undoubtedly have gained new honor in the general distribution of titles. For Macbeth now feels that murder is the only way in which he can achieve the kingship.

Lines 48-58 In his aside Macbeth calls upon the stars to hide their light. What he is contemplating doing should be done only in the darkness, which throughout the play is symbolic of evil. (See "symbol," GLOSSARY-INDEX.) His "black" desires (51), too evil to be seen, should be hidden in darkness. Darkness as setting and as imagery is suggestive of evil throughout the tragedy. (See "setting," GLOSSARY-INDEX.)

Macbeth's image of the eyes' winking upon the work of the hand is expressive both of his intense aversion from the deed and of his intense desire to get what the deed will accomplish. At the same time his "let that be" (52) marks the point at which his fascinated contemplation of the thought of murdering Duncan becomes a resolution, although he will waver from it. The opposition between eye and hand is indicative of the civil war within him.

Ironically unaware of Macbeth's dark thoughts, Duncan, listening to Banquo's praise of Macbeth, says that such praise is a "banquet" (56) to him. Banquets are symbolic at other points in the play of communion and concord—false rather than real—among their participants.

Scene v Lady Macbeth at the castle in Inverness is reading a letter from her husband that tells of his encounter with the witches. She comments that he is ambitious but has too many scruples. At this moment a messenger arrives to inform her that Duncan will be there that very night. She calls upon evil spirits to render her devoid of compunction. Her soliloquy indicates that, although she is guided by the philosophy that there is no such thing as crime, only weakness, she is not so unnatural as to be without human feeling. Her husband arriving on the scene, she hails him by his present and future greatness and, observing his agitated countenance, tells him to hide the thoughts which are disturbing him.

COMMENTARY: *Lines 1-31* We are to take Macbeth's letter as written during a stop on his way from the heath to Duncan's palace. His "my dearest partner in greatness" (11-12) indicates his excited elation at the prophecy as well as his love for his wife, but he does not say that he proposes to do anything to achieve that prophecy.

Lady Macbeth comments shrewdly on her husband's character although in her own excitement she exaggerates what appear to her to be his weaknesses and minimizes what appear to her to be his strengths. She says that he is "not without ambition" (20), but we have seen that he is burning with ambition. She says that he is without the ruthlessness which should accompany ambition, but we have seen him contemplating murder and resolving upon it. Nevertheless he does have scruples which stand in the way of his committing murder. The series of antitheses which she uses to describe him are appropriate in their presentation of the spiritual wrestlings that go on within him before he is vanquished by evil. (See "antithesis," GLOSSARY-INDEX.)

Lady Macbeth's values are an inversion of ordinary human values. The conventional virtues are reasons for reproach. She fears Macbeth's nature, not because it is cruel, but on the contrary because it is "too full o' th' milk of human kindness" (18). "Human kindness" means both "those qualities peculiar to mankind" and "compassion," for compassion is absorbed by babies with their mothers' milk so that it becomes a part of their very being. Macbeth has too much of ordinary human nature in him to "catch the nearest way" (18), even though it means passing over human bodies. He was able to hew his way through the Norwegian ranks to reach the Norwegian commander, but he is not ready to do so where killing is unsanctioned by duty.

For Lady Macbeth, however, greatness consists of being above consideration for the scruples of the general run of men. Ambition, and with it the will-power to gain one's goal, is the highest virtue. "Milk o' human kindness," as far as she is concerned, is a contemptuous allusion to the proverb that milk is a food for infants while meat is the food for men. To have too much of the milk of human kindness is to be what we would call a milksop. Similarly, Lady Macbeth is scornful of the desire to act "holily" (22), like a saint incapable of living in the real world of men.

Lines 31-55 "No compunctious visitings of nature" (46) are to prevent her from doing what she has to do. Here as elsewhere the word "nature" is significant. It implies that the feeling of pity is instinctive. Lady Macbeth is aware that she has the capacity for pity, and this is why she is impelled to call upon evil spirits. She is not a monster; she only wants to become one.

She asks the spirits attendant upon murder to take the milk from her breasts and substitute gall. "Milk" here, as in "milk o' human kindness" and throughout the play, signifies the sweet, gentle qualities of human nature, and gall signifies black, bitter inhuman cruelty. Yet, although compassion is shown to be natural, evil, which disregards all compassion, is omnipresent in the world of *Macbeth*. Paradoxically, although present throughout nature, it is monstrous and unnatural. Although it is immediately and intuitively perceived as contrary to nature, it comes unbidden into men's thoughts, as it did in Macbeth's. "Mortal thoughts" may thus mean not only thoughts which are deadly but thoughts which are mortal because they are characteristic of mortal men, who are prone to sin.

Lady Macbeth concludes her soliloquy by invoking night. Night is to come with a blackness so "thick" (51), so deep, that Heaven will not be able to "peep," as with the eye of a single star, through the "blanket" in which it is enshrouded. This parallels Macbeth's previous calling upon the stars to hide their light. Macbeth had wanted that "the eye wink upon the hand," but Lady Macbeth desires that even the knife itself should not see the wound it makes.

The words "knife," "pall," "dark," and "hell" were closely associated with each other in many passages in Elizabethan literature dealing with the stage. When tragedy was to be performed, the stage was hung with black and the stars represented on the roof of the stage ("the heavens") were blotted out. "Blanket," in addition to the pall in which the figure of tragedy was traditionally represented as enshrouded, suggests a sleeping world, oblivious to the workings of evil. The "murthering ministers" are "sightless," that is, invisible. Evil is present everywhere although unseen, but its deepest affinity is towards the blackness of night. The passage grows out of a traditional concept of tragedy as concerned with affrighting evil, darkness, and hell.

Lines 55-74 Lady Macbeth is as if possessed. Indeed, Elizabethans would have believed that she was literally possessed by the evil spirits whom she had summoned. She greets the entering Macbeth (54-55) by his two present titles and, without naming it, by his title of the future. The threefold greeting and the "all hail" echo the greeting of Macbeth by the witches. She has been "transported" (57), she says, swept forward in time as in a vision beyond "this ignorant present," the present which is ignorant of the future. As was true of Macbeth, she feels her vision of the future to be intensely real. Whereas Macbeth, however, had recoiled with horror from his vision of his murder of Duncan, she speaks with exultation. Her vision of Macbeth as king proves indeed to be real, but in another sense it proves to be a deceitful appearance. Instead of the kingship's bringing them supreme joy, it brings them the utmost torment.

For Lady Macbeth at this moment, however, the murder of Duncan is "this night's great business" (69); it is a heroic enterprise "which shall to all our nights and days to come/Give solely sovereign sway and masterdom" (70-71). The sonorousness of the last line, with its alliterative *s*'s calling to be heavily emphasized and its culmination in the triumphant "masterdom," is expressive of her elation over their future monarchical power. But human beings, particularly those in the grip of evil, are deceived concerning the future. Macbeth's and Lady Macbeth's days—and even more, their nights—are to be given over to anguished restlessness, not the satisfaction of the exercise of power.

The only power Lady Macbeth is to exercise is that over her husband at this very moment and in scene vii. Carried away with herself, she assumes mastery for the time being over her husband, telling him that she will take care of everything. Murder is unspecified but understood between them.

In referring to it, she makes use of word-play that conveys in its grim humor her half-suppressed exultation. Her lines imply that she will "take care of" Duncan in a different way from their obvious meaning, through murder, and it will be done with "dispatch" ("efficient quickness and speed").

Scene vi Duncan on his arrival finds Macbeth's castle to be pleasantly situated. He greets Lady Macbeth, who has come to receive him, and inquires about Macbeth. "I appreciate the love which attends me," Duncan says playfully, "even though it is sometimes a nuisance. In the same way you should be grateful for my love, as shown by this visit, even though it has put you to an inconvenience. You should accordingly pray to God to reward me for this troublesome favor." Lady Macbeth gives the proper reply: "We are devoted to the prayers you ask of us."

COMMENTARY: *Lines 1-10* Duncan's remarks about the pleasantness of the atmosphere surrounding the castle where he is to be murdered are dramatically ironic. Banquo's reply (3-10) contains words and images of love and procreation ("loved," "wooingly," "bed," "procreant cradle," "breed") together with those of religious associations ("temple-haunting," "heaven's breath"). The suggestion is that the castle, placed in the midst of nature, is a place of the natural feelings that tie men together—love, devotion, reverence. Banquo too is ironically mistaken. The castle is a place of unnatural evil. The croak of the raven, a bird of ill omen, to which Lady Macbeth refers on hearing the news of Duncan's coming (I,v.39-41), more appropriately suggests its atmosphere.

Lines 10-31 There is probably an implied comparison between Duncan and Christ in the exchange between the King and Lady Macbeth. Such comparisons were frequently made use of in Elizabethan literature to illustrate the idea that the best conduct is that which is most imitative of Christ. Christ was represented as the supreme example of love in his giving himself up for mankind, of whom he asked nothing more than that it love him in return, as Duncan asks Lady Macbeth to do and as she falsely states she will do. Lady Macbeth adds that everything that Macbeth and she possess is really Duncan's, to be accounted for whenever he wishes. Her words are a ceremonious statement of feudal vassalage, but "compt" was frequently used to refer to the accounting at the Day of Judgment, and the statement may have a further meaning, of which she is unaware: Macbeth and she are disregarding their debt to Christ, to whom mankind owes everything, and are forgetful of the great reckoning to be held at their death.

Scene vii Macbeth, overcome by his thoughts, has left the banquet hall before the ceremonial supper for Duncan is over. Alone, he gives voice to his feeling concerning the rashness and the awfulness of the projected murder. He gives three reasons for not performing the murder, in the order of ascending climax: it would be imprudent; it would violate the blood-tie of a kinsman, the allegiance of a subject, and the duty of a host; and Duncan has been so blameless a king that to kill him would be monstrous. The culmination of Macbeth's speech is a visualization of the entire world weeping for his victim. Lady Macbeth, worried by his absence, enters and reproaches him for having left the chamber. When Macbeth tells her that they will not go through with the murder, she accuses him of not loving her and of lacking manhood. She goes on to say that she has known the tenderness of nursing a child, but if she had sworn as he had done to perform the deed she would have dashed the baby's brains out before she violated her oath. Her words show that she is not without womanly feelings, for she has experienced a mother's love, but she violently suppresses these feelings and implicitly calls upon Macbeth to suppress compassion, "the milk o' human kindness," as unworthy of a man. She prevails over him, and he admiringly exclaims that her spirit is such that she should bear only boys. They cannot fail, she adds, if they summon up enough courage. Duncan will be sound asleep as a result of his hard day's riding, and she will see to it that his two grooms of the bedchamber will have been so plied with liquor that they will be in a drunken sleep. He exclaims in admiration of her and proposes that they use the daggers of the two men and smear the men themselves with blood so that suspicion will fall on them. She agrees, and host and hostess return to their royal guest with smiling faces of hospitality.

COMMENTARY: *Lines 1-28* In his opening statement concerning the imprudence of the murder, Macbeth says that if he could be sure of the consequences here on earth he would take a chance on the next world. His very phrasing of the idea indicates the desperate courage with which, lured by a great attraction, he regards the risk. Life is conceived of as a bank or sandbar on the verge of being covered by the ocean of eternity, and the risk of an after-life is a frantic leap into the unknown. Later, when Macbeth speaks of Duncan's virtues, however, he refers definitely to the "deep damnation" (20) entailed for the murderer.

The irony is that he is right in both instances. He will get the retribution here on earth of which he speaks, his own actions and words turning against him. As one of his nobles says at the conclusion (V, ii,18), the revolts springing up all about him will remind him of his own breach of faith in murdering Duncan. He will also be aware that he has given up his immortal soul to Satan (III,i,68-69). It would have been well if Macbeth had paid heed to his own words instead of accepting the philosophy that the extraordinary man can make his own law and his own future, secure against the consequences of his violation of natural law. The theme of the future, its relation to the present, to one's actions, to the possibility of foreseeing it through supernatural aid or intuition, is one of the main themes of the play. Macbeth here foresees it accurately, as Lady Macbeth had not.

Lines 28-82 Another important theme is the theme of what constitutes a true man. It is here introduced in the dramatic exchange between Macbeth and his wife. To her taunt of cowardice, he replies in effect (46-47) that murder is inhuman and not a sign of manliness. Lady Macbeth replies that he was a man when he suggested the idea of murder and that if he would only do now what he had before dared to talk about, he would be even more of a man. The great opportunity which has come to him has only acted to "unmake" (54) him, to undo his manhood. That Lady Macbeth has a man's spirit, not a woman's, her husband regards as praiseworthy. He does not realize that in having called upon the spirits of evil to unsex her (I,v,41-42) she has become evil and unnatural, just as she is demanding that he become evil and unnatural.

Nevertheless it takes a tremendous effort of the will for him to act in accordance with the concept of what it is to be a true man which he has taken for his own. Macbeth has to exert every power to make every organ of his body obey his will (79-80), for that which he is about to do is so unnatural that there is an internal rebellion within him.

The relation between Macbeth and his wife in this scene is also unnatural, as the Elizabethans would have conceived it. The function of a husband was to rule his family but to rule in love and in reason, as the king rules over his subjects. For the wife to rule is unnatural. Lady Macbeth does not address herself to her husband's reason but to his passions, which should be commanded by his reason—to his pride and to his ambition. She is also implicitly calling upon him to put his love for her before his love for God. In doing so, she is, unthinking of the momentousness of the deed and of the consequences it will have for them and their entire people, like Eve tempting Adam to share her fall. History repeats itself because as a result of the fall of Adam men are prone to sin and consequently constantly repeat the pattern Adam set. We need not accept either the Elizabethans' view of women or their theology to respond to the power of the scene which these overtones help to give it or to perceive that Lady Macbeth is making use of two traditional and powerful wifely weapons: "You don't really love me" and "You are not a man."

Act II

Scene i In a court within the castle Banquo and his son Fleance are walking about. Banquo is disturbed and cannot sleep. He is momentarily startled when he hears some one but relaxes when he finds that it is Macbeth. He tells Macbeth that he dreamt last night of the three witches, but Macbeth pretends that they have been absent from his thoughts. They agree to discuss the significance of the encounter at some other time. When Macbeth speaks vaguely of Banquo's supporting him at the proper time, promising to reward him if he do so, Banquo replies that he will if he can in so doing maintain his blamelessness and his true allegiance to the king.

Macbeth, left alone, awaits the sound of the bell which is to be the signal that the preparations for the murder of Duncan have been completed. As he waits, it seems to him that there before him is an air-borne dagger that moves towards Duncan's bed-chamber and, as he looks upon it, becomes covered with blood. Awful visions fill his mind. The bell sounds, and he proceeds measuredly and stealthily up the staircase leading to Duncan's chamber.

COMMENTARY: *Lines 1-32* Banquo is unable to sleep because the powers of evil are seeking to work upon him. It is after midnight—the witching hour—and there are no stars in the darkness (4-5), as Macbeth had previously wished.

Until the last act, when there is a restoration of light, the scenes are predominantly to be set in darkness. The "fog and filthy air" of the witches—the obscuration of daylight—has been succeeded by pitch blackness.

Banquo continues to be a contrast to Macbeth. He too is visited by temptation, but he calls upon heaven to help him to resist "the cursed thoughts that nature/ Gives way to in repose!" (8-9). Human nature gives way to evil dreams in sleep because evil is in human nature as well as all around it. However, also in human nature is reason, which enables us to control our evil impulses. In this world of evil we cannot afford to relax our resistance to it for a moment. But Banquo is staunchly loyal to the king. While Macbeth uses "honour" (26) to mean distinction, Banquo uses it to mean the merit that deserves such distinction, without which such distinction is false.

The inception of this encounter between the true thane and the false thane is dramatically ironic: Banquo, who has given his sword to Fleance, acting as his squire, calls for it when, tense as he is, he hears a sound. He is reassured when he sees that the noise was made by his host—but his first impulse was right.

Lines 33-64 The vision of the dagger illustrates once more the power of Macbeth's imagination. It is also another playing upon the theme of the difference between appearance and reality. It recedes from him as he seeks to grasp it, leading him in the direction of Duncan's room. It seems as real as his own dagger, which he now draws, but he cannot touch it. Are his eyes deluded while his other senses are true—another instance of the conflict between Macbeth's senses—or do they perceive something which has a reality unapprehended by his other senses?

Macbeth addresses the dagger floating in the air as "fatal vision" (36). It is a vision showing what seems to him to have been sent by fate to lead him to the sleeping Duncan, a vision that will be fatal to Duncan. Macbeth is as if in the grip of the future. He follows the dagger as if he were a sleepwalker moving without his volition. The hour is one in which over the entire hemisphere "Nature seems dead, and wicked dreams abuse/ The curtained sleep." There is no sound or motion. Everything seems to be dead. Only evil dreams which deceive the sleepers seem to be real, and he himself seems to be in such a dream as he "moves" with "stealthy pace" "like a ghost" (54-56). In the awful silence he looks upon himself as if he were disengaged from his own body, a spirit looking upon a body proceeding towards its awful task as if it were walking in a dream. The sound of the bell—one of the many effective noises either heard off-stage or suggested in the imagery during the action immediately before, during, and after the murder—breaks the silence and rouses him to perform his terrible deed.

Scene ii Lady Macbeth is waiting tensely for her husband to commit the murder. Keyed up, she hears the owl's shriek, which was supposed to portend death and which she hence compares to the bellman or town-crier who was sent to toll his bell in front of the prison on the night of the execution of a condemned criminal. She envisages Macbeth killing Duncan. She would have killed him herself, she reveals with a humanizing touch, if he had not resembled her father as he slept. There is a cry from outside the room, and she is for a moment afraid that the two grooms have awaked and the attempt has been unsuccessful. Nothing happens, however, and after a few instants Macbeth enters. After having committed the murder, he passed a room in which a man, roused from his sleep by a dream, called out "Murder!" awakening his companion. It was Donalbain, one of the king's sons, and his attendant. Macbeth had to stand outside of the door waiting for them to go to sleep again before he could continue. One of them cried "God bless us!" but Macbeth could not give the automatic reply to a blessing, for the word "Amen" stuck in his throat. It seemed to him that he heard a voice proclaiming that, since he had murdered sleep, he would sleep no more. Lady Macbeth urges him to come to himself and to wash the blood off his hands. Noticing the daggers in his hands, she asks him why has he brought them and tells him to take them back and to smear the faces of the drugged grooms with blood. He cannot bring himself to return, and she goes to perform the task. A knocking at the gate startles Macbeth, and he wishes that it could rouse Duncan, but time cannot be rolled back. On Lady Macbeth's return, the knocking continuing, she hurries him off to get the blood off his hands and to change into a dressing-gown. It must seem as if they have been roused from sleep.

COMMENTARY: *Lines 1-14* The murder takes place off-stage. The sight of Duncan being killed would have alienated our sympathy from Macbeth and Lady Macbeth. We have to see through their eyes and to hear through their ears in order to share their terror and horror.

Lines 14-57 The strange sounds off-stage alternate with tense silences. Macbeth never answers Lady Macbeth's question (17), first replying with a number of questions indicative of his confusion and then, distracted by an imaginary noise, which causes him to listen strainedly, forgetting it and addressing her with another question of his own. It was he, having thought he heard a voice, whom she had heard call out. The cross-questions suggest their extreme tension.

Lady Macbeth's unimaginative practicality and her skeptical rationalism contrast with Macbeth's visionary imagination. When he tells her of the voice that had three times said he would sleep no more (41-43), the three forms of address echoing the witches' greetings of him, she asks "Who was it that thus cried," as if it could only have been the voice of an identifiable person. For her, Macbeth's dwelling on what he has heard is simply thinking "brainsickly" (46), a contemptuous synonym for "insanely." She says in a dramatically ironic foreshadowing of her eventual mental collapse that such thoughts will make them mad. She is not afraid to go back to plant the daggers by the drugged grooms and the dead Duncan: "The sleeping, and the dead,/ Are but as pictures; 'Tis the eye of childhood/ That fears a painted devil" (54-55). In other words, she is saying: "Don't be a child; be a man," as though manhood consists of being superior to conscience and religious dreads.

Lines 57-74 Macbeth, looking upon his "hangsman's hands" (27)—hangsmen had such tasks as disemboweling living persons—refers to his wife's telling him to wash "this filthy witness" (47) off his hands. For her the blood is merely evidence to be got rid of, physically repulsive, but nothing more. For him it is symbolic of his guilt, which he can never get rid of. The entire ocean will not wash his hand clean. As he horrifiedly regards his hand, he imagines its red slowly turning the green of the ocean to crimson. This celebrated image is the most powerful of the blood images, as his statement that his hands will "pluck out mine eyes" (59) is the most powerful of the images of conflict between parts of the body.

Macbeth's fascinated contemplation of his hands is treated contemptuously by Lady Macbeth, who has returned with bloody hands of her own. "A little water clears us of this deed" (67), she tells him in words that are perhaps reminiscent of Pontius Pilate. She urges him not to be lost in his thought "so poorly," that is, in such a poor-spirited way, and he, rousing himself, replies that it would be better for him to be unconscious forever rather than to have to be continually conscious of his crime.

Scene iii A porter, who has been carousing during the night, goes to open the gate at which there is a knocking. He grumbles as he goes to answer the insistent summons and, the thought occurring to him that the porter at hell-gate must be even busier than he, he indulges in a whimsical pretence of being that porter, making believe that he is admitting various sinners. Finally, he admits the noblemen Macduff and Lennox. Macduff has been asked by Duncan to call upon him early in the morning. Macbeth enters in his dressing-gown to greet them. He stands talking to Lennox as Macduff goes to wake the king. Lennox asks whether the king is leaving that day. "He does," replies Macbeth, but corrects himself guiltily. "He did appoint so." Lennox then passes the time, as people do in such circumstances, by talking of the weather. Lennox's talk, however, is not ordinary chit-chat. In his whole life, he says, he has never experienced such a night. Nature was profoundly disturbed. Chimneys were blown down, the earth seemed to shake, there were continuous owl-screechings and strange screams. Such unnatural happenings were supposed to accompany the death of kings. Macbeth, however, merely replies with constrained understatement: "'Twas a rough night." Macduff returns crying out in horror, and Macbeth and Lennox hasten to Duncan's room while Macduff orders the alarm-bell to be rung. Lady Macbeth, Banquo, and Malcolm and Donalbain rush in one after another, and Macbeth and Lennox return. In the midst of the expressions of horror and dismay, Macbeth tells the company that, carried away by rage at the evidently guilty grooms, he killed them. Lady Macbeth faints and is carried away. The members of the company agree to return to their rooms to get dressed and then to meet to inquire further into the crime. Malcolm and Donalbain remain. They express their fear and suspicion of their kinsmen and decide that it would be safest for them if each were to flee to a different haven, Malcolm to England and Donalbain to Ireland.

COMMENTARY: *Lines 1-47* The comic interlude of the porter serves a number of purposes. It is dramatically necessary to fill the interval while Macbeth and Lady Macbeth go to change their clothes. The contrast between the porter's bleary-eyed grumbling return to his normal workaday routine after a night's carousing and the pretense of Macbeth of awakening to ordinary, everyday reality after his unknown night of horror is ironic. Even more ironic is the fact that the porter's whimsy of being keeper of hell-gate is more true than he realizes: it is indeed a hell into which the castle of Macbeth has been transformed by his awful deed. In bringing us back to the normal world, the porter makes us realize this more sharply. His jesting acts as a relief from extreme tension, but it is thematically significant.

When the knocking at the gate had first started, it had appalled Macbeth, not because he had feared being detected but because it seemed, like the other sounds and voices he had heard, terrifyingly ominous. Indeed it was. Macbeth did not know it, but the person doing the knocking was Macduff, who has been born to kill him. The knocking was as the sound of fate. With the entrance of the porter the knocking, which had given such urgency to the action of Lady Macbeth in the scene before, becomes the signal of the return to normality. With the coming of day, life is re-commencing and resuming its natural course.

But normality is always followed by new abnormalities. Life at all times is subject to the promptings of evil. The porter's jokes about the familiar things of the day would have universalized the murder for the Elizabethans. His admission to hell of the "equivocator" is a grimly ironic reference to the very recent Gunpowder Plot, which had shocked England greatly. Some of the participants in this conspiracy (see COMPLETE BACKGROUND, Shakespeare's England–Contemporary Events) were Jesuits, who adhered to the doctrine that under duress one may swear to statements made with mental reservations or deceptive ambiguities. The porter's comment would therefore have linked this would-be treasonable murder with that of the distant past being enacted on the stage and suggested that the struggle with evil goes on everlastingly. Macbeth, it should be noted, having falsely played the part of a welcoming host, has from now on to deceive, to utter words which he does not mean, but he too cannot equivocate to heaven. He himself will be deceived by the witches, of whose "equivocation" (V,v,43) he is to learn when he finds that their words of seeming reassurance have another meaning.

Lines 48-68 The conversation that Macbeth engages in before the discovery of the murder is loaded with dramatic irony. He is addressed by conventional titles of courtesy–"noble Sir" (49) and "worthy Thane" (50)–but in the circumstances these serve as a comment on what Macbeth has done: it was ignoble, not noble, and anything but worthy of a thane toward his king. Beneath the exchange with Macduff are similar ironies.

Lines 69-101 Macduff, like Macbeth, but for different reasons, finds the sight of the dead Duncan too terrible to look upon. It is "the great doom's image" (83), a sight as awful as the Day of Judgment. Duncan's death is a prefiguration of the time of universal death, as the sleep from which Macduff is calling Malcolm, Donalbain, and Banquo to rouse themselves, is "death's counterfeit" (81).

Everyone is aroused by the clanging of the alarm-bell, used in the times of direst emergencies to summon men to arms. To Lady Macbeth's question as to the reason for the summons, Macduff, addressing her as "gentle lady," says that it is not for a woman to hear (90-91). The words are doubly ironic in view of her call to be unsexed and Macbeth's praise of her masculine courage.

Macbeth's profession of grief is also dramatically ironic. If he had died an hour before Duncan, he says (96-101), he would have lived a happy life, but from now on there is nothing worthwhile left. This is not merely a lament for Duncan, expressed in conventional terms, which Macbeth delivers in continuing to play his part, although it is that. It also has a significance of which the others are unaware, expressing his overwhelming consciousness of sin.

Lines 102-152 Lady Macbeth's swoon, sometimes thought to be pretended, is probably genuine. She screwed her courage to the sticking-point, but now that everything has gone through as planned, she relaxes the tension of her will and collapses.

Scene iv An old man and Ross, standing outside Macbeth's castle, discuss the strange natural phenomena that have taken place. Macduff enters and gives them the latest news. It has been decided that the two grooms killed Duncan, and, since Malcolm and Donalbain ran away, apparently because of guilty fear, it is believed that the grooms were in their pay. Macbeth has been chosen king and is to be crowned at Scone. Macduff, who is not going to the coronation, expresses uneasiness about the future.

COMMENTARY: ***Lines 1-20*** The unnamed old man is a person of rank and dignity who has seen many strange things in his life and has the wisdom of age. He acts as a choric commentator. (See "choric," GLOSSARY-INDEX.) His conversation with Ross points up the strangeness of recent events. The word "strange," used by the old man (3) and reiterated by Ross (14), signifies the unnatural. It occurs frequently in the course of the play.

Ross asks (8-10) whether the darkness in mid-day they are experiencing is caused by Night's having gained the ascendancy over Day or by Day's hiding itself in shame over the guilt of man. The antithesis between day and night, here as elsewhere, is linked up with the antithesis between good and evil and that between order and chaos. Has evil triumphed, or is good only temporarily in abeyance? Are we witnessing the end of things?

The idea of the possible end of things is suggested more strongly in Ross's immediately preceding words (5-6): "Thou seest the heavens, as troubled with man's act,/ Threatens his bloody stage." This makes use of the common idea of the time that the world is a stage, with man the actor in a play and God the spectator. It suggests that God is looking on and shows his anger by the eclipse, which is a threat of the coming of the Day of Judgment. "Heavens" is not merely a synonym for God; it has a theatrical meaning. In the Elizabethan theater the roof of the stage, bespangled with stars, was called the "heavens." "Act" similarly means primarily "deed," but it also refers to the division of a play. It is noteworthy also that the Elizabethan stage was draped with black when a tragedy was being shown. The theatrical terms have the effect of universalizing the evil committed by Macbeth: what the audience is witnessing as it watches the tragedy of *Macbeth*—and the audience is reminded that it is watching a stage representation by the imagery and diction—is the tragedy of mankind itself.

Lines 21-41 The terseness with which Macduff replies to Ross in giving the "official" theory of the crime indicates some holding back in accepting it. It was Macduff, it will be remembered, who in the previous scene asked Macbeth why he killed the grooms. In telling Ross that he will not attend the coronation, he expresses the hope that the coronation will really be for the good of the country. He does not have any definite suspicions, but he is uneasy.

The old man's couplet, which concludes the scene, is spoken with something of a seer's vision. Uttered to himself as Macduff and Ross have turned to leave, he calls down a blessing on those persons who, not knowing where evil lies, are ready to accept as friends those who mean no good. The words act as a warning of things to come, but they are also an assurance that good, though deceived by evil, will finally triumph.

Act III

Scene i Banquo comments that all of the predictions of the witches have proved true for Macbeth but that he fears that Macbeth has engaged in foul play to make this so. Nevertheless, since they prophesied that he will be the father of kings, he has reason to hope. Just then, the trumpets announce the coming of Macbeth, now king, and his court. Macbeth reminds Banquo of that evening's feast, at which Banquo is to be the chief guest. While paying compliments to Banquo and talking to him about a council meeting to be held the next day, Macbeth slips in three questions: "Ride you this afternoon?", "Is't far you ride?", and "Goes Fleance with you?" These are what he is really concerned with in the conversation. We learn of their significance a little later. Dismissing his court, Macbeth sends for two men who are waiting outside the palace gate at his command. While he is waiting for them to arrive, Macbeth expresses in soliloquy his fear of Banquo, whose valor and ability promise that the witches' prophecy concerning him will be fulfilled. If so, Macbeth will have incurred damnation only for the descendants of Banquo. The murderers entering, Macbeth reminds them of a previous conversation in which he had explained to them that it was Banquo who had been the cause of troubles which had befallen them. He asks them if they are ready to let their wrongs go by unavenged, and, on being assured that they are not, informs them that Banquo is also his enemy. They can both avenge themselves and gain his favor by waylaying Banquo and his son Fleance. He will send word to them within an hour as to where to station themselves.

COMMENTARY: *Lines 1-43* Banquo has been thought by some critics to be acquiescing here in Macbeth's accession and becoming an accessory to the murder after the fact as a result of ambition. It is doubtful, however, that Shakespeare would have portrayed James I's ancestor thus unfavorably. Banquo suspects Macbeth, but there is nothing that he can do at the moment. In fact, it is uncertain that there is anything that he could properly do, since in the officially promulgated political theory, it was sinful to conspire or rebel against any king, even one who had ascended the throne wrongly. The insurrection against Macbeth at the end is an exception, so horrible are Macbeth's crimes, but at this moment Macbeth has not yet proved himself an absolute tyrant. Ambition would have caused Banquo to proceed against Macbeth, as Macbeth had proceeded against Duncan, to try to realize the witches' prophecy. He is, however, content to bide his time, secure in the belief that the future is governed by God's plan, which will work itself out.

Lines 44-72 Macbeth had regarded the kingship as the height of human desire. Ironically, however, he finds no pleasure in it. He now thinks that if only he can get rid of Banquo, he will rest secure, but this is only a self-delusion, for his fears multiply. Macbeth will never feel secure, for he knows that the crown is not rightfully his. He lives in the knowledge that he has killed a king and fears that he has taught others a lesson in doing so. Despairing of the next world, he devotes himself entirely to securing his safety in this world. From now on, he is resolute in seeking this end.

In speaking of his fears of Banquo, Macbeth pays him an involuntary tribute. Banquo, he says, is of a regal nature and is both courageous and prudent. We remember the soliloquy in which Macbeth told himself that it would be imprudent as well as immoral to kill Duncan. Banquo is neither.

In his expression of disillusionment Macbeth uses images of infertility: he has acquired a "fruitless crown" (61) and a "barren sceptre" (62). This is appropriate, for evil is destructive and sterile rather than creative and life-giving. Since Lady Macbeth, in giving herself to evil, had asked to be unsexed, Macbeth cannot be "father to a line of kings" (60).

In referring to Banquo, however, Macbeth makes use of an image of fertility: the "seed of Banquo" will be kings (70). So Banquo in his soliloquy had said that the witches had stated that he would be the "root and father/ Of many kings" (5-6). In previous scenes (I, iv, and vi), Banquo has also employed images of fertility. The opposition between Macbeth and Banquo, between the unnatural and the natural, the sterile and the fertile, continues throughout. Rather than accept the idea of Banquo's being father to a line of kings, Macbeth tries to fight against the future.

Lines 73-142 The two men to whom Macbeth speaks are not professional murderers, as are the brutal hirelings whom Macbeth later employs to kill Lady Macduff and her son. They are ruined gentlemen who in their desperation are ready to do anything. They had thought their troubles came from Macbeth, as we are to suppose that in fact they did, but he has convinced them that they come from Banquo. Once again, we have the impression of the inability of men to distinguish the evil from the good.

Macbeth employs with them arguments similar to those which Lady Macbeth had employed with him. If they are "not i' th' worst rank of manhood" (103), he tells them, they will revenge themselves on Banquo. The implication is that there is an order of manliness and that revengeful murderers stand in the front ranks of this order. "Bounteous Nature" (98) has established such an order among men, as she has among dogs. But the order of which Macbeth speaks is a reversal of natural order, and the concept of manhood contained in it is a false concept.

With the same scorn that Lady Macbeth showed in disposing of his moral objections he sweeps aside the idea of Christian forgiveness and of the acceptance of the world's misfortunes as God's will. The first ruined gentleman, speaking for both, accepts the view that men with the passions of men and not the spiritlessness of milksops will take revenge.

Scene ii Lady Macbeth shares her husband's sense of insecurity and his fear of Banquo. The scene begins as the previous one had ended, with the word "Banquo." The servant's statement to her that Banquo will return that night underscores the irony of Banquo's previous assurance to that effect: although dead, Banquo will indeed return that night in a form that will be more frightening to Macbeth than ever. The conversation between Macbeth and his wife reveals a change of relationship between them. Macbeth addresses her as lovingly as before, but he has taken charge and plotted on his own to kill Banquo. He hints of it to Lady Macbeth but does not divulge it to her. She, in turn, no longer addresses him scornfully but tries to comfort his tortured mind. In a weak repetition of her previous advice she hints that Banquo and Fleance are mortal and can therefore be killed and urges him not to reveal his thoughts in his face and his manner at the supper that night. In a similar repetition of his previous apostrophe to Night, Macbeth calls upon it to sew up "the tender eye of pitiful Day" (46-47), as the eyes of falcons were sewn up to deprive them of sight and make them tractable, and with its "bloody and invisible hand" (48) to tear up the bond between fate and Banquo. As if in response to his summons, night begins to fall, and Macbeth looking out upon it again imagines all of nature falling asleep while "Night's black agents" rouse themselves once more.

COMMENTARY: Although Macbeth and his wife seem superficially to have been drawn closer together by the crime in which they have participated, we see the beginnings of an alienation between them. She asks him why he stays by himself, making as his companions his miserable thoughts and imaginings (8-9). Alienated from mankind by his crime, Macbeth is to be increasingly alienated from his wife. He lives alone in his tormented inner world, of which his images of torture (he refers to a mental torture rack in ll. 21-22 and says in l. 36 that his mind is "full of scorpions," swarming and stinging) give indication. She in her turn, after expressing her fear of Banquo, feels it imperative on his entrance to hide her anxiety.

Both Lady Macbeth and Macbeth express envy of Duncan in his grave. Macbeth underscores the irony. To gain peace, he has sent Duncan to his peace while he lies in torment on his sleepless bed. Life for Macbeth is a "fitful fever" (23), from which there is rest only in death. In another disease image he speaks of the "affliction" of his "terrible dreams," which "shake" him nightly (17-19). The prophecy of the voice which cried that he would sleep no more has been fulfilled.

Macbeth is suffering a poetically appropriate retribution. He killed the sleeping Duncan; therefore, he cannot sleep. He feasted Duncan before killing him; therefore, he is condemned to "eat our meal in fear" (17). He has played the hypocritical host, and he must continue to do so, dissimulating despite his internal torment at the ceremonial supper he is about to hold. In an image of universal disorder (16) Macbeth states that he would rather that the world fell to pieces, indeed that both heaven and earth be destroyed, than that he continue to suffer as he does.

Scene iii The two murderers have been joined by a third, sent by Macbeth. They await the coming of Banquo and Fleance in a park that has a road leading to the palace. Banquo and Fleance dismount off-stage and come walking along the road. The murderers dash out the torch and kill Banquo, but Fleance gets away in the darkness.

COMMENTARY: The third murderer has been sent by Macbeth, who has a tyrant's distrust of his agents. The two murderers were at first suspicious of the newcomer, but he has convinced them by repeating the preliminary instruction Macbeth has given them. In the world of evil no one can be sure of anyone.

Because it is evil, the world of *Macbeth* is a world of danger. The belated traveller spurs to get to the inn before nightfall because it is dangerous to ride abroad at night. So does Banquo, the last of the guests to arrive for the supper. The palace is, however, no harbor for him. Less than a mile from it he is killed.

Banquo's conversational remark about the weather—"It will rain tonight" (16)—indicates that he is unprepared and that the night is starless, a fit night for murder. The grimly humorous comment on this remark by the first murderer—"Let it come down"—as they rain a storm of blows at him indicates the fierce delight with which they take a supposed revenge. The solicitude of the dying Banquo for his son, as he urges him to escape, contrasts with their ferocity.

Scene iv The guests are assembled for the banquet. Macbeth leaves for a moment to speak to the first murderer at the door. He is elated by the news of Banquo's death, but his elation is dashed when he learns that Fleance has escaped. Returning to the feast, he resumes his role as gracious host and expresses his regret at the absence of Banquo. At this moment he sees the ghost of Banquo seated in his own place at the head of the table. He speaks wildly to it, and Lady Macbeth expostulates with him. Lady Macbeth in urging Macbeth to regain his self-command at this crucial moment makes use of her previous arguments and her previous scornful tone. She speaks as a disbeliever in the supernatural: it's only his imagination. His conduct is unbecoming a man, she asserts. It is folly that unmans him because what he sees can only be a delusion derived from the womanish credulity that accepts old wives' tales. The ghost disappears, and Macbeth momentarily recovers himself. When Macbeth, however, again states his wish that Banquo were here, the ghost reappears. Macbeth confronts it with words similar to those he had used in defending himself against his wife when they were discussing the murder of Duncan: "What man dare, I dare" (99). He raves on wildly, and the ghost once more disappears. This time, however, the guests cannot contain their agitation, and when Ross addresses a question to Macbeth, Lady Macbeth hurriedly dismisses them. Macbeth, left alone with Lady Macbeth, voices his horror, but then he determinedly recovers his self-control and turns to something concrete: the danger which Macduff, who has refused to come to the feast, poses. He announces his purpose of repairing to the witches to learn more of what awaits him in the future and of continuing in his way of crime in his effort to render himself secure.

COMMENTARY: *Lines 1-32* Each of the first three speeches of Macbeth and Lady Macbeth ends with the word "welcome." Everything is done in proper ceremonial manner. Macbeth invites the nobles to seat themselves according to their degrees. Order is being observed—but it is soon to be broken. When Lady Macbeth dismisses the company, she says (119), "Stand not upon the order of your going."

Speaking to the murderer, Macbeth is elatedly jocular. When he hears, however, that Fleance has escaped, he finds the fever which Fleance's death was supposed to cure returning again. He comments that if Fleance would have been killed, he would have been in perfect health. Macbeth thus continually deludes himself: one more murder, and everything will be well. Nevertheless he momentarily reassures himself with the thought that, regardless of the future, Fleance is no danger at present.

Lines 32-121 The ghost of Banquo is not an hallucination. Ghosts were thought to have the power to render themselves visible only to the person whom they wished to see them. That this ghost was intended to be real is indicated by the stage direction concerning its appearance in the original text. A ghost having existence only in Macbeth's fevered imagination would not have been given bodily form.

Lines 122-144 Lady Macbeth's brief replies to Macbeth indicate that, the crisis past, she is overcome by fatigue as a result of the strain. Macbeth, after brooding for a moment over thoughts of supernatural retribution, abruptly comes to himself, signalling his return to the here and now by asking her what time it is. He is determined to continue along his way. He cannot return to the past, he says in his image of wading in blood (136-138), but must attain his goal of security through more crime and more blood. Further crime, he thinks, will harden him against fear and obliterate the horrible visions which by the conclusion of the scene he has come to believe are imagined by him. The last line signifies that he will cease to be a fearful novice with childish terrors and will become mature, a man, in crime.

At the very time in which Macbeth expresses his determination to perpetrate new crimes, however, there is a hint of the first streaks of a new dawn. Mention of Macduff carries an unconscious symbolic significance, for it is he who is to bring about the dawn, immediately afterwards.

Scene v Hecate rebukes the witches for having dealt with Macbeth without calling upon her. She will distill a vaporous drop on the moon and from it raise false visions which will deceive Macbeth.

COMMENTARY: This scene is a non-Shakespearean interpolation. Including a song written by Thomas Middleton, its iambic meter opposes the trochaic meter of Shakespeare's witches and dispels the atmosphere of foulness and grotesque unnaturalness.

Scene vi Lennox speaks ironically to another lord about the official theory that Malcolm and Donalbain had had Duncan killed, saying that no doubt Fleance had done the same with his father Banquo. We are told that Macduff has gone to England, where Malcolm has been received by the British king, Edward the Confessor, to ask that an army be levied against Macbeth.

COMMENTARY: Macbeth, tormented by his conscience but unable give up the crown and repent, has revealed himself as a tyrant. The people of Scotland cannot eat and sleep in peace (33-35). A king creates a kingdom in his own image, and Macbeth, unable to eat and sleep in quiet, has caused the same to be true of his country. However, we see an opposition developing and a force being assembled in England.

Act IV

Scene i The witches, in a dark cave in the middle of which is a boiling cauldron, throw loathsome ingredients into the hellish stew. Hecate and three other witches enter, engage in song, and leave. Macbeth enters and demands to know the answers to his questions. The witches produce an apparition, an armed head, which anticipates his question and tells him to beware of Macduff. Then they produce a second apparition, a bloody child, which tells him that no man born of woman can harm him. Macbeth, elated, says that to make assurance doubly sure he will nevertheless have Macduff killed. Finally, the witches produce a third apparition, a child crowned with a tree in his hand, who tells him that he will never be vanquished until great Birnam Wood shall come against him to high Dunsinane Hill. Macbeth, still more elated, now demands to know whether Banquo's issue will ever reign. There appears a procession of eight kings, the last with a mirror in his hand, with Banquo, bloody as before, following. In the magic mirror of the eighth king, Macbeth sees many more kings, some with two-fold orbs and treble sceptres. Banquo smilingly points the kings out as his. The witches then mockingly dance about and vanish. Macbeth, dismayed, calls Lennox from where he has been standing guard before the cave to ask him whether he saw them pass. Lennox has not, but he gives Macbeth the news that Macduff has fled to England. Macbeth resolves that from now on he will do immediately whatever terrible thing comes to his mind and begins by deciding to put Lady Macduff and her children to death.

COMMENTARY: *Lines 1-47* This scene is a grotesque parody of old women bending over their cooking. They are making a good, thick gruel, but the objects in it are repulsive and unnatural. Hecate's speech is generally believed to be another interpolation from Middleton, as is indicated by the iambic metre and the ineptness of the comparison of Shakespeare's "secret, black, and midnight hags" (48) to "elves and fairies in a ring" (42).

Lines 48-135 Macbeth's conjuration is an invocation of chaos. Though the whole world be destroyed, he wishes that the future be revealed to him. He cares not for the achievements of man: religion, commerce, agriculture, architecture, and present and past civilizations generally ("palaces, and pyramids" [57]). The culmination is his willingness that "Nature's germens tumble all together" (59), that is, that the seeds from which everything in the future is to gain existence be tumbled together in confusion, producing barrenness or monstrosities. These are the same elemental seeds to which Banquo referred when he spoke of "the seeds of time" (I,iii,58), but Banquo assumed that these seeds would grow in accordance with a divine plan. Here is another contrast between Macbeth the destroyer and Banquo the creator.

The armed head represents Macduff as the soldier whom Macbeth knows him to be and as he will appear, as Macbeth does not know, in the battle in which Macduff is to kill him. The apparition tells Macbeth what he already believes, that he should beware Macduff, just as in Macbeth's first encounter with the witches the first witch, in greeting him as the Thane of Glamis, told him what he already knew.

The bloody child represents Macduff untimely ripped from his mother's womb. Macbeth does not know this but the fact already exists as the fated means of Macbeth's death. This fact corresponds to the greeting of Macbeth as Thane of Cawdor by the second witch, something which was already true but of which he did not have knowledge. But Macbeth hopes to bind fate by killing Macduff, for then fate would have to violate not just one but two of its own laws if Macduff were to destroy Macbeth: the law of birth, that man is born of woman, and the law of death, that dead men cannot regain bodily existence and mortal power.

The child crowned with a tree in his hand represents Malcolm triumphant as king, with the branch of Birnam Wood in his hand which he had ordered his soldiers to carry. This is the event which will take place in the future, of which Macbeth does not know. It is the future which Macbeth seeks to suppress in its babyhood but which inevitably grows to its full power. Macbeth exultantly accepts the apparition's prophecy that he need not fear rebellion, for this implies that he will live the term of life allotted by nature and die of old age. He, who has outraged nature, thinks to die a natural death, but as is indicated by the child with the tree in his hand, nature itself will rise against him.

The witches and the apparitions they summon have throughout refused to elaborate on what they have said, tantalizing Macbeth even as they have voiced their predictions. Now, when Macbeth asks about Banquo's issue, they reply with one voice, "Seek to know no more." It is a sure way to lure him to inquire further. They now show him a spectacle designed to grieve his heart. It is a spectacle that undoubtedly gladdened the heart of Shakespeare's king and appealed to the patriotism of the audience, for James I, who succeeded Elizabeth after having been James VI of Scotland, was supposed to be of the line of Banquo. The kings shown in the magic mirror represent the monarchs who will rule after James over England and Scotland, it is implied, until the end of the world.

The speech of the first witch (125-132) and the dance are probably another interpolation. The speech is in iambic meter, and it would have been more effective for the witches to vanish when he turns to them with the question "What! is this so?" (124). The witches always mockingly leave their beguiled victim unsatisfied.

Lines 135-156 Macbeth's furious exclamation that all those who trust the witches should be damned (139) is a curse that returns upon himself, for after this outburst he does continue to trust them, more and more in desperation. The news that Macduff has fled to England serves in Macbeth's mind to confirm the predictions, for already the warning that he should beware Macduff is proving true. Time, he cries out (144), has forestalled the terrible actions that he was going to perform. In killing Duncan, Macbeth was seeking to speed up time, to make it yield that which had been promised him. Now it seems to him that he is in a race against time. He has to act immediately once an idea comes to his mind lest time deprive him of the opportunity to put it into effect. The sound of galloping horses which he heard (139-140), one of a number of images of rapid riding in the play which contribute to a sense of goaded swiftness, here perhaps suggests the onrush of time as well as the sound of the witches' horses.

The language in which he expresses his resolution to put his thoughts into action immediately is significant. The first purposes his heart may form (147-48) will be the first things his hands will do. Evil is his only first-born, the only thing he can hatch; otherwise, he is barren. Also, it should be noted that there is now no internal war within him: what his heart wishes, his hand does. But this is at the price of the suppression within himself of his moral sense, which caused his body to revolt against what he thought to do.

Macbeth, despite his sense of time operating against him, is unaware of the forces that are gathering and that will hem him in. Lennox, who has been standing guard and who tells him of Macduff's escape, is, we have seen, secretly sympathetic to Macduff and opposed to Macbeth. This is the last time we see Macbeth together with anyone whom we have previously seen in the play, even Lady Macbeth, until he is killed by Macduff. He is terribly and utterly alone.

Scene ii Lady Macduff is complaining to Ross about her husband's flight, which she considers imprudent and a sign of his lack of concern for her and their children. She complains that he must be lacking in the feeling of love for his family natural to all things, for even the wren, the smallest of birds, will fight the owl to protect her young. Ross assures her that Macduff did what was best for him to do. His reply gives us a picture of what Scotland has become under Macbeth. The feverishness and convulsions of the time indicate how the "fitful fever" of Macbeth has spread throughout the kingdom, for a country is healthy only as its ruler is. Like Macbeth, the people are beset with fears, fears that spring from rumors, which in turn originate from fears. In a land dominated by fear, one cannot tell what is true and what is false. The disorder image is reminiscent of the sailor's ship that was tempest-tossed by the witch. After Ross leaves, Lady Macduff and her son engage in some sad joking. A messenger, risking his life by his coming and expressing pity for Lady Macduff and her children, enters to warn her to fly with her children immediately. Before she can do so, however, Macbeth's hired ruffians arrive. They kill the boy and run after her to kill her off-stage.

COMMENTARY: *Lines 1-29* This is a scene of pathos which relieves the terror that has been so predominant in this tragedy. Instead of participating in the nightmares of Macbeth, we witness the pitiful suffering and destruction of his innocent victims.

Lady Macduff's love for her children makes her upbraid her husband for his flight. We are to understand, however, that Macduff conceived it as his duty to his country to join Malcolm and seek the aid of England even though it might entail some risk to his family, whom he could not believe even Macbeth would slaughter. The owl, the bird of death, alluded to by Lady Macduff, should be associated with Macbeth because it shrieked all the night of the murder of Duncan. Thus it is not Macduff who is unnatural, but Macbeth.

Lines 30-64 The cleverness of Lady Macduff's son has the charm of childhood precociousness, a charm which may come off better on the stage than in reading, where it may seem rather artificial. Pathos and humor mingle, the mother's sadness and her commiseration for her defenseless son being balanced by the boy's delightful assurance in his wit. Dominating the dialogue is the audience's awareness that Macbeth has given orders that the castle be surprised and they killed. The boy's smart retort to his mother's calling him a poor bird, that traps are not set for such poor birds as he, and the joke about her marrying again are dramatically ironic in the light of this awareness.

Lines 65-85 In the presence of these murderers the pathetic, grieving woman and upbraiding wife becomes the great noblewoman proudly defiant in behalf of her lord. She, who had been implying that her husband is dead to her, tells the murderers that she hopes that her husband is "in no place so unsanctified" (81)—the words recall that Macduff is in the court of the "most pious" and "holy" Edward the Confessor (III,vi,27,30)—that such as they can reach him. Similarly, the boy, who had replied jestingly to Lady Macduff's statement that his father is a traitor—she meant that he had broken his marriage vow to protect her—replies indignantly to the same statement by the murderer. Affectionate to his mother, he is also high-spirited, and he dies bravely, calling upon his mother to run away after he himself has received his death-wound. As in the Banquo murder scene, where Banquo's dying words were that Fleance run away, the brutality of the murderers is contrasted with the tenderness and self-sacrifice of family love.

The murder of Lady Macduff and her son is the turning-point. (See "turning-point," GLOSSARY-INDEX.) It sets the seal on Macbeth as a tyrant and sets into motion the force that will destroy him. The angry and contemptuous words of the murderer to the son of Macduff—"egg," that is, unhatched chick, and "young fry" or spawn of treachery (82-83)—is significant in this connection. These are images of fertility. Macbeth, turned totally to destruction, is trying to strike at the future while it is yet in the seed, but nothing can prevent the future, the consequences of his own acts, from happening. In fact, he only hastens that future.

Scene iii In England Macduff urges Malcolm to lead an expedition against Macbeth. Malcolm, however, is suspicious of Macduff, as Macbeth had previously sent secret agents to him seeking to entice him to return to Scotland. He is convinced of Macduff's sincerity when, as a ruse to see Macduff's response, he falsely accuses himself of being so vice-ridden that he will be an even worse king than Macbeth. When Macduff turns away in passionate indignation and sorrow, Malcolm tells him the truth. Moreover, he informs him that an English army has already been gathered to invade Scotland on behalf of Malcolm. While Macduff is standing amazed at the good turn of events, Malcolm speaks to a doctor, who tells him that King Edward has been delayed because, with his miraculous power of curing the disease of scrofula by touching its victim, he has been detained by a horde of sufferers of the disease. Ross enters with fresh news of Scotland. He tells them that Scotland is in a worse plight than ever and, after some hesitation, tells Macduff of the slaughter of his wife and children. Macduff resolves to execute vengeance on the field of battle, and Malcolm expresses his certitude that they will triumph with the aid of heaven.

COMMENTARY: *Lines 1-139* This lengthy, discursive scene, sometimes regarded as too drawn out, furnishes a respite in the swift-moving action and presents a choric commentary on the evil of Macbeth, touching on a number of themes of the play.

Malcolm justifies his suspicion of Macduff by stating the difficulty of knowing where good is and where evil is when evil assumes the form of good. Yet despite the deceptiveness of evil in assuming the guise of good, good must maintain its own appearance. The difficulty in distinguishing between appearance and reality is increased by the fact that good may be corrupted into evil. Macbeth "was once thought honest" (13), just as the brightest of the angels, Lucifer, also fell (22).

Macbeth is thus identified with Lucifer, whose fall through ambition in seeking to supplant God set the pattern for evil human behavior. He is also spoken of as "black Macbeth" (52) and "devilish Macbeth" (117), and it is said of him that in the legions of hell there is not a "devil more damn'd/ In evils" (55-57) than he. Malcolm, on the other hand, is implicitly compared to Christ. He says that Macduff may think it politic to make a sacrificial offering of him, "a weak, poor, innocent lamb," in order to appease Macbeth, "an angry god" (16-17). The lamb is a symbol of Christ, and the angry god is one of the pagan gods who were thought to have become the devils of Christian theology.

When Malcolm speaks of his alleged vices, he reverses the actuality. He lists the kingly virtues to say that he does not have them, but it is in Macbeth that they are absent. His supposed disregard for "the sweet milk of concord" (l. 98) recalls that Macbeth once had the "milk o' human kindness." But whereas Macbeth has brought disorder to Scotland, Malcolm, in reverse of his statement, will not. To test Macduff. Malcolm says that, compared with himself, Macbeth will seem to everyone to have been a lamb (54). Good, taking a cue from evil, has disguised itself to test good, just as evil, using deception, tempts those who may be prone to it.

Lines 139-159 The description of Edward the Confessor opposes the saintly king of England to the devilish king of Scotland. Edward's "heavenly gift of prophecy" (157) is a supernatural power derived from heaven in contrast with the power of the witches derived from hell. His miraculous cures contrast with the hurts which Macbeth inflicts upon Scotland. Again and again, Scotland has been personified and described as beaten down, driven, wounded, and bleeding (3-4, 31, 39-41). Macduff had asked when will Scotland see "wholesome days" (105) again. The answer is when it gains a king "full of grace" (159), as Edward is.

Lines 159-240 The theme of what constitutes a man is once more played upon when Macduff is informed of the murder of his wife and children. Malcolm urges him to struggle against his grief "like a man" (220); Macduff replies, "I shall do so;/ But I must also feel it as a man" (220-221). The gentler feelings of pity, love, and grief are as much a part of manhood as anger and courage. Macduff tempers his grief and contains his anger, resolving to seek revenge. This revenge, however, is a revenge on the field of battle by one whom the murder of his wife and children has made the symbol of outraged Scotland and an agent of divine justice.

Malcolm at the end of the scene states that God's angels are urging them on. His last line uses the recurring night-day antithesis, this time as a promise that Scotland is about to emerge out of the night which Macbeth has brought upon her.

Act V

Scene i Lady Macbeth's waiting gentlewoman recapitulates to a physician at the castle on Dunsinane Hill what she has witnessed. During this period, when Macbeth has been busy taking action against rebellion, she has seen Lady Macbeth walk in her sleep. As they are talking, Lady Macbeth enters sleepwalking. She speaks aloud, re-living the nights Duncan and Banquo were murdered and trying desperately to wipe imaginary blood off her hands. When she thinks that she has finally got them clean at last and raises them to her face to look at them more closely, she smells the odor of the blood and realizes that she can never rid herself of the remembrance of the crime. The physician and the gentlewoman look on in horror as Lady Macbeth betrays herself. When Lady Macbeth returns to bed, the physician comments that she needs a clergyman more than a doctor and orders the gentlewoman to remove from Lady Macbeth anything which she might use to inflict harm upon herself.

COMMENTARY: The previous long scene gives the impression that a good deal of time has gone by since we last saw Lady Macbeth. Although, when she spoke to Macbeth at her last appearance, her nerve was strong, we have seen indications of the strain upon her. Her breakdown has therefore been prepared for.

The scene is in prose except for the doctor's concluding lines, which act as a choric commentary and bring the scene to an effective conclusion. Prose is the appropriate medium for the rest of the scene, as the regularity of meter would not befit Lady Macbeth's disjointed utterances. Moreover, the simple language of the gentlewoman, expressing the awed horror of ordinary persons in the face of a revealed monstrous evil, and the clinical, if similarly horrified, observations of the doctor are best couched in prose.

The presence of the doctor on the scene recalls the doctor in England who could not explain on the basis of scientific knowledge Edward's miraculous cures. So too this doctor states: "This disease is beyond my practice" (65). It is a matter of a sick soul rather than a sick body, and Lady Macbeth needs the divine rather than the physician (82). Matters concerned with the supernatural are in each instance beyond the ken of science. The supernatural, however, affects the natural.

The sleepwalking is highly dramatic in its revelation of that within Lady Macbeth which she had sought to suppress and also highly ironic. She had called upon night to come to hide her deed, but now she is afraid of the dark and has light by her when she goes to sleep. She had told Macbeth that a little water would clear them of the deed, but now in her sleep she continually washes her hands, seeking to get the blood off them. The shock which she received on going back to Duncan with the bloody daggers, a shock which she successfully suppressed, is revealed in her terrible question "Yet who would have thought the old man to have had so much blood in him?" (44-45).

Many of her sentences repeat or echo with ironic effect what she had said before. Compare ll. 42-43 with I,vii,77; or ll. 49-50 with her contemptuous "O, these flaws and starts" (III,iv,63) at the banquet scene. But at this very moment she is revealing her guilt, as she had rebuked Macbeth for doing. She repeats her command to Macbeth at the time of the Duncan murder to wash his hands, but she herself is now trying in vain to wash her own hands. Her "What's done cannot be undone" (75) echoes her previous "What's done is done" (III,ii,12), but then she was saying to her husband that there is no point in thinking about the past, which cannot be changed. Now the words have the ring of despair: the horrible past cannot indeed be changed, nor can one escape from it. Finally, her concluding words remind us not only of Macduff's knocking at the gate when she told Macbeth that they must go to their bedroom to change their clothes; they remind us that Macbeth cannot sleep in his bed and that she cannot find true rest in sleep.

Scene ii An army led by the Scotch nobles Menteith, Caithness, Angus, and Lennox is marching near Birnam Wood to join the English army led by Malcolm, Siward, an old English general, and Macduff. The news is that Macbeth is fortifying Dunsinane Castle in a mad frenzy. Many are coming over to the rebels, and those who serve under Macbeth do so unwillingly.

COMMENTARY: This is the first of a number of short scenes in this act, which alternates between the opposition and Macbeth. On the modern stage, where the curtain goes down after each scene so that scenery may be changed, such short scenes offer problems and may cause the action to lag. The Elizabethan stage, however, had no elaborate scenery and no curtain. Each scene followed immediately after the preceding one, making possible swift-moving action and emphasizing the contrast between scenes. We alternate between Macbeth's frenzied defiance and the opposition's confident patriotism.

The Scotch nobles continue the imagery of disease to indicate the life-giving qualities of the opposition to Macbeth. The wrongs of Malcolm and Macduff would stir a paralytic to action (3-5). Macbeth is said to be "mad" (13) and "cannot buckle his distemper'd cause/ Within the belt of rule" (15-16). Here we have a figure that is at once a disease image ("distemper'd" means swollen with dropsy), a clothing image, and a disorder image. A succeeding clothing image (20-22) suggests a picture not of a bloated Macbeth but of a dwindling Macbeth, evil falling away in the presence of advancing good. His "pester'd" (23) or tormented mind behaves erratically. Malcolm is the "med'cine" (27) of the sick country. His men are ready to shed their last drop of blood as a "purge" (28) for Scotland's illness. Blood here is life-giving, unlike the blood which Angus speaks of as "sticking" on Macbeth's hands (17).

This revolt, though good, must, it is stated, remind Macbeth of his own breach of faith (18). The invasion from without and the aid it receives from within are also reminiscent of the Norwegian invasion aided by the Thane of Cawdor which Macbeth had put down at the beginning of the play. Here, however, the reigning monarch is an absolute tyrant and the one opposing him is the rightful heir to the throne. Moreover, the joining together of the English and Scotch forces foreshadows the later organic union of the United Kingdom and is therefore proper.

Scene iii Macbeth at Dunsinane is in a frenzy about the defection of his thanes, but he holds to the belief that no rebellion against him can succeed until Birnam Wood comes to Dunsinane. He rages when he hears about the English force and orders his armor to be put on so that he may be in readiness for battle. The doctor tells him that Lady Macbeth is not physically ill but deeply troubled mentally. When he tells Macbeth that for such mental illness there is nothing he can do, Macbeth replies furiously. Speaking impatiently to his squire, talking first about his wife's illness and then about the illness of Scotland, he is distracted.

COMMENTARY: In the preceding scene reference to Birnam Wood and Dunsinane reminded us of the apparition's prediction, to which we see Macbeth now clinging in desperation. Also, the description of Macbeth has prepared us for his outburst at the frightened servant and his impatience with his squire. He commands him to put his armor on him even though it is not yet time for battle and the armor will tire him, is fretful when the squire is not as fast as he wishes, and leaves before a piece of armor has been put on.

In the midst of his frenzy he betrays a weariness with life. When he asks the doctor whether he cannot erase thoughts deeply imprinted in the brain or relieve the oppressed heart by some drug that will confer the sweetness of utter forgetfulness (43), he reveals his own tormented conscience and his longing for peace, the peace which he had given Duncan. In another speech he says, "I have liv'd long enough: my way of life/ Is fall'n into the sere, the yellow leaf" (22-23). Actually, an analysis of the time scheme shows that there has been no lapse of years, but Shakespeare, in what has been called "double time," often gives an impression of the passage of time at variance with the reality. Here the impression is that Macbeth has endured a lifetime of suffering. Moreover, in his old age he cannot expect that which should accompany old age—there is an implicit contrast here with the old age of Duncan—such as honor, love, obedience, friends. In his loneliness he is aware of the precious human values he has given up, and this awareness helps to maintain some sympathy for him. Yet, lonely though he be, he continues to fight with the courage of despair, a courage that echoes and yet contrasts with his courage at the beginning of the play.

The soul weariness and the frenzy of Macbeth are expressed in continued disease imagery. Although he holds himself to be immune from the sickness of fear, he does admit for a moment that he is "sick at heart" when he perceives his isolation. Nevertheless a little later he states that success in the battle will "cheer me ever" (21). He is still deceiving himself, thinking as always that one more thing will make him happy. He is equally blind when he speaks of the disease of Scotland (50-56), not realizing that he is the source of it.

Scene iv Malcolm orders his troops to hack off the boughs of Birnam Wood to bear in front of them, thus obscuring the number of men from Macbeth's scouts. The news that Malcolm and his generals have received is that Macbeth, seeing that he is losing men to the enemy and doubtful of those remaining, has resolved not to give battle but to withstand a siege in well-fortified and well-provisioned Dunsinane.

COMMENTARY: We see now how Birnam Wood will come to Dunsinane and wait to see how Macbeth will be killed although this cannot be done by a man born of woman. The solving of the riddles helps to maintain interest as the inevitable conclusion approaches.

Scene v Macbeth proclaims that he will wait out the invading forces, who must succumb to the famine and pestilence that attends a siege. Just then, a cry of women is heard. On inquiry he learns that Lady Macbeth is dead. He responds without grief, soliloquizing on the meaninglessness of life. The future is without any significance. It is not anything to be striven for or prevented, for nothing in life is worth fighting for. Lady Macbeth would have died sometime in the future if she had not died now, and it makes no difference just when, for each "tomorrow" is a step, no different from the one before or after on the monotonous course toward the grave. When a messenger comes in to say that he has seen Birnam Wood moving, Macbeth, on finding the seemingly impossible prediction coming true, orders his men out: at least, they will die fighting.

COMMENTARY: The cry of the women, which once would have caused the chill of terror, now does not even startle Macbeth. He has become inured to terror, a man at last, according to the criterion of manliness he has accepted. The irony is that in having become such a man he has become drained of all feeling so that he receives the death of his wife, who had taught him this concept of manliness, with the indifference of apathy. He has become alienated, has come to feel that life is meaningless and futile.

In Macbeth's famous soliloquy, once more life is compared to a drama on the stage, this time, however, to convey the sense of its brevity, transcience, and illusoriness. In saying "Life's but a walking shadow" (24), Macbeth is echoing the Bible, but not to contrast the insubstantiality of life on earth with the glory of God or the life hereafter: for him life ends in "dusty death" (23). "Shadow" suggests "actor," for actors were often spoken of as shadows, mere imitations of life. Life is a "poor player," for the actor, no matter with what violence of passion he conducts himself, finds his little time on the stage soon over and he himself only a rapidly disappearing memory. Just so with life itself; the real thing is just as transitory as the imitation. Even more horrible and pathetic, it is not even a coherent work of art; it is rather like the wild, confused babbling of an idiot, a story without a meaning. This is what Macbeth has finally come to feel: behind the appearance of order in life is the ultimate reality—nothingness. All of his passionate strivings have been for naught.

This is a powerful and disturbing view of life, but we see it as the consequence of Macbeth's having severed himself from mankind. As it is being expressed, we see the forces of order on the march. The Scotch nobles would gladly give up their lives for their cause. It is the sense of being engaged in a collective human enterprise that makes life have meaning.

Macbeth, however, though weary of life, intends to go on fighting. He is ready to destroy the entire universe with himself. This extraordinary egotism is all that he has left. Aghast by the messenger's news that Birnam Wood seems to be moving towards Dunsinane, he nevertheless orders his men to leave the castle to engage in hand-to-hand combat. Disregarding his own previous words that he can withstand a siege, he thus ironically causes the prophecies to come true. Proceeding in desperation, he as always brings his destruction upon himself.

Scene vi On a plain before the castle, Malcolm commands his men to lay down their boughs, for they have come close enough. He marshalls the order of battle.

COMMENTARY: Good has hidden itself, but now it shows itself as it is. Malcolm's command to his army that it proceed "according to our order" (6) contrasts Malcolm as the representative of order with Macbeth as the representative of disorder.

Scene vii Macbeth, fighting desperately, confronts Young Siward, the son of the English general, and kills him. Macbeth takes this as assurance that no man born of woman can harm him. As he leaves the stage, Macduff enters, looking for him, and hearing a great noise off-stage, indicating that a great warrior is fighting there, follows it. Malcolm and old Siward enter, and we learn that the castle has been given up by Macbeth's men, who are really on the side of Malcolm.

COMMENTARY: Macbeth seems to know that he must die and fights with the desperation of a wounded animal, comparing himself to a bear beset by dogs in the Elizabethan sport of bear-baiting. Yet even now, after so many deceptions by the powers of evil, he clings to the prophecy that he cannot be hurt by a man born of woman. His slaying of Young Siward, who has met him undaunted, even though he regards Macbeth as a diabolical figure, encourages him to continue. At this final moment he seems invincible.

Macduff, in proclaiming that he will fight with none but Macbeth, reminds us that as the symbol of outraged Scotland he is the person destined to kill Macbeth. His reference to the "wretched Kernes" (17), Irish freebooters and irregulars, with whom he will not fight, recalls the "merciless Macdonwald" (I,ii,9), who also employed these mercenaries. Disorder has repeated itself and will again be quelled.

Scene viii Macduff, coming upon Macbeth, tells him to turn and fight. Macbeth does not wish to do so, saying that he has too much of Macduff's blood upon him already, and tells Macduff that it is no use for Macduff to try to kill him, as no man born of woman can hurt him. When Macduff replies that Macbeth should despair of his charm protecting him, for Macduff was "from his mother's womb/ Untimely ripp'd," Macbeth is for a moment daunted and refuses to fight. On being told, however, that he will be made captive to be exhibited to the populace as a monster, he determines to fight to the end and is driven off-stage. Malcolm, entering, expresses concern at the absence of Macduff and Young Siward. Ross informs Siward that his son died on the field of battle. Siward, on learning that his son died bravely, says that he could not have died better and gives him up to God. Macduff enters with Macbeth's head mounted on a pole and hails Malcolm as king of Scotland, a cry taken up by all. Malcolm rewards his friends by making them earls, the first of that title in Scotland, and, promising to do everything necessary to set the kingdom to rights, invites every one to witness his coronation at Scone. Lady Macbeth, he announces parenthetically, died, apparently by suicide.

COMMENTARY: *Lines 1-34* Macbeth rejects the idea of imitating the ancient Romans, who thought it a point of honor to commit suicide when faced with overwhelming odds, thus triumphing in a sense over their opponents. With animal ferocity, he wishes to kill as long as he sees opposing soldiers. The epithet "Hell-hound" (3) which Macduff uses in addressing him combines an animal image with a diabolical image.

Macduff's announcement of how he came into the world is portentous. It is as if, a bloody prodigy of Nature, he was prematurely called into being to meet the harsh needs of the time. He is the bloody child, once pitiably weak, who is now terrifyingly invincible.

Macbeth's reluctance to fight Macduff is caused in good part by the prophecy "Beware Macduff." Nevertheless, his statement that there is too much of Macduff's blood on him already must be accepted, for it is in keeping with his expressed wish to the doctor that certain memories could be extirpated from the brain. Here, as in his expression of his desolation in his later years, we see that, despite the epithets directed at him, he has not quite lost all his humanity. Terrible in his isolation, he does not leave the stage without the audience's feeling some sense of loss for the extinguished glory of this figure of darkness. His fear of Macduff, the fear of a moment, is caused by a sense of helplessness at having been deserted by fate. However, he summons up his resolution and dies with satanic defiance.

COMMENTARY: *Lines 35-75* Some editors print this scene as a continuation of the previous scene rather than a new one, with a gathering on the field of battle to the flourish of trumpets. Others, however, print it as a separate scene, with Malcolm remaining in the castle.

Siward's son, we were told earlier (V,ii ,9-11), was one of many young men who proclaimed that they had come to manhood by joining the army. These young men are representative of the future which Macbeth had sought to suppress. Their rising up against Macbeth, like the rising of Birnam Wood, is indicative of Nature itself, violated by Macbeth, moving to expel him. Young Siward only lived until he proved himself to be a man in battle and then "like a man he died" (43).It was not only, however, his personal courage that established his manhood but his acting as "God's soldier" (47) in doing his patriotic duty.

Malcolm, surrounded by his "kingdom's pearl" (56), occupies the proper place of a king, the center of things. His proclamation of his thanes as earls suggests the beginning of a new epoch in which there is a greater social stability with a more sharply defined social hierarchy. It recalls Duncan's promise that when Malcolm will be invested with his title "signs of nobleness, like stars, shall shine/ On all deservers" (I,iv,41-42). Malcolm uses the same imagery of nature's bounty (65) as did Duncan. His promise that whatever is necessary to be done will be done "in measure, time, and place" (73) is a promise of the restoration of order.

CRITICAL ANALYSIS

Viewed superficially, *Macbeth* is a drama with the theme "Crime does not pay." It is that, but it is much more than that. One of the things that make it more than that is that it is concerned with no ordinary criminals. The prize they seek is great, the temptation is unusual, the crime is most heinous, and they themselves have capacities that are in certain respects extraordinary. The distance between the delight in the exercise of power they expect and the agony they suffer is tremendous. Yet, although everything is heightened in this world of the poetic imagination, everything is convincingly real.

We feel toward them and their catastrophe more than the fascination and the awe with which we witness the extraordinary. We sympathize with them. It may seem strange to say that we identify ourselves with one who is a murderer of women and children, but it is true. Shakespeare makes us feel what it is to be a Macbeth, makes us share his terrors and his desperation. And even though the courage which had first aroused our admiration is used to enable him to continue in his course despite the tortures inflicted on him by his conscience, it remains admirable, as does the strength of the conscience which he is never quite able to crush.

Even at the conclusion Macbeth never quite forfeits our complete sympathy. The memory of what he was and his own regret for the human values he has lost makes him more than the diabolical figure or the trapped animal which he is regarded as being by his opponents, although he is that too. Through him we have seen the potentialities of human nature for good and for evil. That he brought his own downfall upon himself only heightens the tragic effect, for we are aware how narrow is the margin between saving one's self and losing one's self, how terribly a part of him fought against that in him which led him to his downfall, how much he himself cast away—and yet how difficult it was for him not to do so.

We cannot, therefore, simply say, "It serves him right." His satanic defiance at the end elicits a horrified admiration. We acquiesce in the retribution which overtakes him, for, even though we identify ourselves with Macbeth, we are also able to stand outside of him and see the consequences of his action inevitably destroying him. Realizing, however, the great human qualities which have been devastated in the course of the drama, our response is a complex one that includes a sense of waste. To put it in the very simplest terms, it includes such feelings as "How awful" as well as "It had to be."

Because the hero is a criminal, *Macbeth,* one of the world's great tragedies, violates many of the critical clichés about tragedy. We are told that the tragic hero must be a good man with a flaw of character, but a man who wantonly kills women and children can scarcely be called good. We are told that the tragic hero gains a dearly earned self-knowledge, but Macbeth continues to deceive himself up to the end, thinking that one more successful murder or one more successful battle will make him happy. We are told the tragic hero's defeat is also in some sense a triumph, but it would be hard to claim that Macbeth triumphs in any way. What we can say is that, even though Macbeth is not a "good" man and even though his downfall is not a mingled triumph and defeat, we do receive from his catastrophe the sense of the glory and dignity of man which we get from the downfall of the more conventional tragic hero. We get too the kind of perception concerning him and the human situation which the hero himself in other tragedies often gets.

Because Macbeth is the kind of hero that he is, he evokes less pity than the tragic hero often does. King Lear is a majestic figure, but in the course of the tragedy we see him as a "foolish fond old man" who arouses our tenderest feelings as he learns the meaning of love from his daughter Cordelia. Othello too is a commanding person, but, as Iago brings him low, we feel that his words, "The pity of it, Iago," apply to himself as much as to Desdemona. Not so with Macbeth.

Yet the tragedy in which he appears is not devoid of pathos. It is most evident when we witness the calamities that come to the innocent victims of Macbeth. In the scene in which Lady Macduff and her son are murdered, we do not put ourselves in their places and share the terror that besets them. We look upon it as a piteous spectacle irradiated by the beauty of the mother's love and the charm of the boy's precocious cleverness. The simple, wholesome domestic feelings come as a relief from the great passions of Macbeth and Lady Macbeth.

We also, however, even feel something of pity for these two towering figures in the face of their agony and desolation, although this pity is of a grudging, sterner sort. When, as Macbeth feveredly speaks of new murders, Lady Macbeth replies wearily, "You lack the season of all natures, sleep," we appreciate her solicitude for him and perceive her own unvoiced misery. If she had dissolved into self-pity with some such statement as "If only I could get a good night's sleep!" her grandeur and that of the tragedy would have been shattered. But the implied statement and her concern for him humanizes her and evokes some pity even as her stoicism in suffering maintains her stature.

The doctor observing Lady Macbeth's sleepwalking acts as a choric guide to our response. "God, God forgive us all!" he exclaims. Predominant in these words is the feeling of horror and awe at what he has seen: "The terrible crimes of which human beings are capable! God forgive all of us for the evil within us!" But also present is a sense of pity for poor, suffering, frail humanity: "The tortures which human beings can bring upon themselves! God forgive all of us, for we know not what we do until it is too late!"

For, extraordinary individuals as Macbeth and Lady Macbeth are, they are also representative of humanity. Their situation is the human situation. The evil which engulfs them is the evil which surrounds each of us. Of course, the dramatic universe that is *Macbeth* is not ordinary, everyday life in suburban America. But it is a dramatic and poetic heightening of certain aspects of that life. All of us do things which have unforeseen consequences, and none of us can escape from the past and from ourselves. It might further be argued that *Macbeth* makes us more sharply aware of an essential reality of our time—the memory of genocide and mass slaughter, the alienation, the suppressed terror and violence—that lies beneath the placid surface of things.

This is a function of poetic drama. It presents us not with the surface of things but with a world of the imagination that has significance for us. It is important to remember that *Macbeth* is such a poetic drama. The poetry is not a mere convention or a mere ornament but the medium through which the effect is conveyed. This is why a study of its language and its poetic devices is so rewarding. These devices work their effect upon us even though we are not conscious of them. But if *Macbeth* is poetry, it is also drama. All of the images, symbols, and themes in the world would not make *Macbeth* what it is if it did not create characters who are life-like while greater than life-size. The "Commentary" of the COMPREHENSIVE SUMMARY has sought to take into account that *Macbeth* is neither pure poetry nor pure drama but a poetic drama. In the theater we should not spend our time counting images, but our experience should be enriched by the close reading we have given the play.

CHARACTER ANALYSES

The Two Main Characters and the Dramatic Atmosphere

A discussion of the characters of Macbeth and Lady Macbeth might well begin with the eloquent words of A. C. Bradley: "From this murky background [of the tragedy] stand out the two great terrible figures, who dwarf all the remaining characters of the drama. Both are sublime, and both inspire, far more than the . . . heroes [of Shakespeare's other tragedies], the feeling of awe. They are never detached in imagination from the atmosphere which surrounds them and adds to their grandeur and terror. It is, as it were, continued into their souls. For within them is all we felt without—the darkness of night, lit with the flame of tempest and the hues of blood, and haunted by wild and direful shapes, 'murdering ministers,' spirits of remorse, and maddening visions of peace lost and judgments to come. The way to be untrue to Shakespeare here, as always, is to relax the tension of imagination, to conventionalise, to conceive Macbeth, for example, as a half-hearted criminal, and Lady Macbeth as a whole-hearted fiend."

Macbeth At the beginning of the tragedy, Macbeth is presented as a great warrior of remarkable courage who has just saved his country. He is respected and honored by all. He is, however, a man fired by ambition, which has been further stimulated by his recent triumph. The guilty thoughts with which he has been playing now come to the fore. He responds to the witches because there is something within himself that answers to their evil.

The thought of murder is, however, abhorrent to him. He has a vivid imagination which paints its horrors chillingly. Yet the attraction of power is great. With that attraction is joined the sinister suggestion of the witches, the unexpected frustration of the announcement that Malcolm will be proclaimed heir, and the fact of an unusual opportunity. All of these, however, would not have had sufficient effect to cause him to commit murder if it were not for the goading of his wife. She has extraordinary force of personality, but she would not have been able to succeed in moving him if he were not impelled from within in the same direction and if he were not lacking in self-knowledge. He does not realize that it is the better part of his nature which is speaking to him through the imagination that conjures up before him such terrible visions. Her appeal to his manhood is therefore successful.

Before he goes to kill Duncan, the vision of the dagger leading him to Duncan's chamber and becoming covered with blood as he draws his own dagger fills him with the utmost horror. Yet with a tremendous effort of the will he impels himself to do what he has set out to do. The moment he has performed the deed he is stricken with terror—but it is not the terror of being detected. It is the terror of the consciousness of his guilt. He had proceeded in his crime as if it were a frightful nightmare from whose grip he could not be released, and he had awakened to the sickening realization that the nightmare was reality.

Yet despite the terrors which beset him he has no thought of giving up the crown. As he himself had predicted, his sense of guilt causes him to fear that what he has done others will do to him. He proceeds from crime to crime in a vain search for security, overcoming his terrors with a fearful courage and determination. He steels himself and, whereas at first his terrors were reflected in his face, now he becomes adept at dissimulation.

At the end, hardened to everything, he becomes almost devoid of feeling. He had been closely joined to his wife in love and in a common ambition, but now the news of her death evokes no grief in him. For he has come to find life to be meaningless and futile, a weary and monotonous succession of horrors to whose effect he has become dead. Yet even now he does not remain sunk in apathetic weariness but oscillates between it and a wild frenzy. He fights to the end with the courage of despair.

Lady Macbeth Lady Macbeth is like Macbeth in the strength of her ambition, which is not apart from his, but unlike him in that she is not troubled by imagination. She is hard, practical, and rational, not one to summon up visions. All that matters is the goal and the will-power to achieve it. She therefore sweeps aside moral scruples and the terrors engendered by a moral conscience.

Her will-power and her courage are indeed very great. Having determined that Duncan's visit is their supreme opportunity, she consciously and deliberately suppresses any feeling of compunction within herself. Inspired by what seems to her a moment for greatness, she carries her husband along with her. She shows remarkable self-command in the face of danger at the time of Duncan's murder and at the time of the appearance of Banquo's ghost.

Yet, although she has been governed by her philosophy that the truly great person is above ordinary human morality, she has, almost unknown to herself, an internal resistance to what she is doing. The sleeping Duncan reminds her of her father, and she leaves the murder to her husband. Her calling upon evil spirits to deprive her of any trace of compassion indicates that she has normal human feelings which must be subdued if she is to go on.

She does not have the imagination to anticipate what will happen after the murder, but once it is accomplished she sinks under the strain. Her domination over her husband was only the domination of a moment when she was carried along by the evil spirits she had invoked and he needed her stimulus to plunge ahead. Now, as he is driven on to further crime by the agony within him, she, stricken by the unexpected horror of the deed, which comes as a shock to her, no longer takes the lead.

Only once, when the appearance of Banquo's ghost makes it necessary for her to summon her resources of will to take command of the situation and urge her husband to quell his terror, does she regain her former ascendancy. Once he has done so, she recedes into the background. She seeks to help and comfort him, but his agony and her desolation separates them from each other. Her will remains strong, and she reveals that desolation only in talking in her sleep. It is in keeping with her character that she cuts short her own life.

*Characterization of Others**

The other characters are less highly individualized than most of the characters of comparable importance in Shakespeare's other great dramas. This has the effect of throwing into higher relief the two main characters. They, enveloped in the peculiar atmosphere of the tragedy, dominate it and give it a distinctive grandeur and simplicity that would have been detracted from by the variety afforded by more highly individualized secondary characters.

Banquo Of the other characters, perhaps the most important is Banquo, for he acts as a foil for Macbeth. Banquo is the loyal thane, as Macbeth proves to be the disloyal one. He is the co-commander with Macbeth in battle, and his exploits too are highly praised, although Macbeth is given preeminence. He accompanies Macbeth on the heath, but his response to the witches is direct and straightforward, unlike that of Macbeth, who starts guiltily and commands the witches to speak further. He dreams of the witches on the night that Macbeth kills Duncan, but, unlike Macbeth, he resists thoughts of evil. He is not intoxicated by the witches' prediction of glory, as Macbeth is, but is content to let time work itself out. Macbeth says of him in soliloquy that he is of royal temper. This is befitting the father of kings that Banquo is to be. He is generous and open-hearted, praising Macbeth to Duncan and using the images of fertility that also characterize the benevolent Duncan and that are especially appropriate to the founder of such an enduring dynasty as he is. For further discussion of Banquo, see the COMPREHENSIVE SUMMARY, "Commentary" on I,iii,38-88; II,i1-30; III,i,44-72; III,iii,1-23; IV,i,1-47.

Duncan Duncan is an aged, saintly king, beneficent and overflowing with tenderness. His virtues, his affection for Macbeth, and his lavishness towards Macbeth make his murder especially heinous. He is unsuspecting in his goodness

*The student is referred to the GLOSSARY-INDEX at the end of this guide for a listing of characters with simple identifications and, when not given there, to discussions in the COMPREHENSIVE SUMMARY.

and is deceived by Macbeth as he was by Cawdor. For further discussion of Duncan, see "Commentary" on I,iv,1-47.

Macduff Macduff is the ardent patriot whom destiny has assigned the role of nemesis for Macbeth. His uneasiness and then his suspicion concerning Macbeth gradually deepen. The murder of his wife and children by Macbeth makes Macduff the symbol of outraged Scotland. He tempers his grief to become God's agent in restoring order and health to Scotland. For further discussion of Macduff, see "Commentary" on II,iv, 21-41; IV,iii,159-240.

Malcolm Malcolm is a young man free of all guilt who will be a godly king. He emerges at the end as a figure who stands in contrast to what Macbeth has become, a representative of the kingly virtues rather than a person. For further discussion of Malcolm, see "Commentary" on IV,iii,1-139.

The Other Characters As for the rest, the old man, Lady Macduff, the two doctors, and Lady Macbeth's gentlewoman have their individual traits, although they are flat rather than rounded characters. (See "flat character," GLOSSARY-INDEX.) For further discussion of these characters, see the "Commentary" on the scenes in which they appear—respectively, II,v; IV,ii; V,i. V,i. Angus, Ross, and Lennox are merely representative of the Scotch nobility, first deceived by Macbeth and then rising up against him. Taken together, all of these characters furnish something like a chorus commenting on the action.

STUDY QUESTIONS

The answer to an essay examination question can always be given in a single sentence and can often be given in a book-length treatise. Obviously, the instructor expects neither. He wants an essay as long as the student can reasonably write in the time allotted, an essay that is well organized and coherent, containing as much detail as possible. The detail gives substance to the generalizations and indicates that the student is doing more than repeating memorized formulas. It should, however, be relevant detail whose significance to the topic under discussion is demonstrated. The student accordingly has to make a selection of what is most relevant and most important. He should therefore give himself time to think before he writes.

1. *Discuss the use of dramatic irony in* Macbeth.

Macbeth, a drama in which men act in ignorance of unseen evil forces all around them, is full of dramatic irony, for this ignorance is the occasion of irony. Thus Lady Macbeth and Macbeth look forward to sovereignty as the height of human desire (although he has contrary feelings also), but being king and queen proves to be the height of torment for them. The manifestations of this torment are themselves ironic. Macbeth had killed the sleeping Duncan; therefore, he himself cannot sleep. He had feasted Duncan before killing him; therefore, he must eat in fear. He had played the hypocritical host; therefore, he must continue to do so in agony. Added to Macbeth's torment is the thought that ironically he had labored only for Banquo, since it is his descendants who will be kings.

The words which Lady Macbeth utters in her rationalism prove in retrospect to be ironic, revealing her shallowness and ignorance. For her it is just a matter of getting rid of the evidence—"A little water clears us of this deed"—not of living with a sense of guilt. She does not know how the murder will affect her. In the sleep-walking scene we see her striving in vain to get rid of the sight and the odor of the blood. Her disjointed utterances, repeating what she had said before, are highly ironic. She had tried to make Macbeth forget his crime with the prosaic commonplace "What's done is done," but we see that what is done continues to be re-lived and repeated.

It is not only the guilty pair who say things that are dramatically ironic, for innocent as well as guilty persons speak in ignorance of reality. Immediately after Duncan has said that he could not guess Cawdor's guilt from his face, Macbeth, the new Thane of Cawdor, harboring thoughts of murder, enters to be greeted by Duncan as "worthiest cousin." Standing in front of the castle where he is to be murdered, Duncan says that it is a pleasant place. The porter of Macbeth's castle pretends after the murder that he is the keeper of hell-gate, not realizing how true in a sense his pretence is.

The chief ironies, however, rise from the fact that Macbeth in his desperate continuance in crime deceives himself and allows himself to be deluded by the witches. He thinks that the murder of Banquo will bring him rest, but on the contrary it adds to his terrors. "Fail not our feast," he tells Banquo. Banquo indeed does not fail to attend—as a ghost who makes Macbeth reveal himself. So too Macbeth holds desperately to the three predictions of the witches. The predictions which seemed to promise him security turn out, however, to be an accurate foretelling of his doom.

2. *Discuss the use of darkness as a setting in* Macbeth.

The dialogue reveals that darkness is a setting for most of the scenes in *Macbeth.* The performance on the Elizabethan stage was of course in broad daylight, but the references to night and the stage-properties—the torches in various scenes and the candle held by Lady Macbeth in the sleepwalking scene—called upon the audience to imagine such darkness. The placing of the scenes in darkness is suggestive of the horror and mystery of evil, which Macbeth identifies with the blackness of night.

The witches appear in the "fog and filthy air" of a thunder-storm and meet Macbeth in a similar scene of obscured day-light. Macbeth calls for the pitch blackness of a starless night in which to perform his crime, as does Lady Macbeth. The night of the murder is such a night, as we are told by Banquo, who, walking after midnight, sees the flare of the torch of Macbeth's servant but fails at first to recognize Macbeth. We are reminded of the darkness when Macbeth, about to commit the murder, envisions nature's operations as suspended in the inactivity of night-time while murder and witchcraft hold sway. It is a starless night also when Banquo and Fleance return from their riding, as we learn from Banquo's comment that it will rain. The next moment the torch is dashed out, leaving them in absolute darkness. The banquet scene in which the ghost appears takes place later that night, the torches of the great banquet-hall casting their glare upon the ghost and the affrighted Macbeth. Macbeth meets the witches, it seems, in the darkness of a cavern, where they bend over their cauldron, and Lady Macbeth in her sleepwalking carries a candle, which she, afraid of the darkness, always has by her bed-side.

The only scenes that seem to take place in broad daylight are those in which Duncan, looking at Macbeth's castle, is ironically deceived by its pleasant setting and the scenes at the end of the play in which the invading forces close in upon Macbeth. That the conclusion should be in daylight is appropriate: the long night of Macbeth's reign is over.

3. *Discuss the use of disease imagery in* Macbeth.

Disease imagery is clustered in the latter part of *Macbeth.* The suggestion conveyed by this imagery is that Macbeth, as a usurping tyrant, is the source of an infection which spreads disease throughout Scotland, a disease which can only be remedied by his extirpation and the assumption of the kingship by Malcolm, the physician of the realm.

Macbeth regards life as a "fitful fever." He speaks of himself as shaken by fear and of lying in restless torment, the shivering, tossing, and turning suggesting feverousness. His description of his mind as a torture-rack and as full of scorpions can also be regarded as disease imagery—that is, imagery conveying an impression of physical ill health or bodily pain.

Ross in his dialogue with Lady Macduff speaks of the time as feverish. Kings, both good and bad, were supposed to fashion their countries in their own image, and here we see how the feverishness of the tyrant has infected the country. So too Macduff, telling Malcolm of Scotland's woes, personifies it, speaking of Scotland as wounded, bleeding, driven, and sinking in weariness. A contrast is suggested between Scotland ruled by Macbeth and England ruled by the holy Edward the Confessor. Edward, the possessor of the king's touch, miraculously heals; Macbeth infects and destroys.

The doctor who appears in the scene in England comments that Edward's cures go beyond the knowledge of medical science. In the next scene the doctor who watches Lady Macbeth betraying her sick soul comments similarly that her cure can be effected only by the clergyman, not the doctor. Macbeth points up the parallel between Lady Macbeth and Scotland when he asks the doctor if he can do anything about the sickness of the country or if he can purge it of the English. The irony is that it is the moral sickness of himself and Lady Macbeth which is the cause of his country's illness and that it is the English force commanded by Malcolm which will restore health to the country. So affirm the Scotch nobles going to join this force. They acclaim Malcolm as the medicine for the sick country and state that they are ready to shed their blood as a healing draught for Scotland.

4. *Discuss the theme of the nature of manhood in* Macbeth.

What constitutes a true man is a theme that runs throughout *Macbeth.* For Lady Macbeth a true man is one who sets great goals for himself and is ready to do any thing to achieve these goals. Moral scruples belong only to ordinary men, not the true man, who towers above ordinary beings. Macbeth, she says, is not without ambition, but he has too much of the milk of human kindness, the compassion of which the true man should be devoid. He would achieve his goal "holily," like a saint unacquainted with practical affairs.

It is by an appeal to his manhood that she prevails over her husband. When he stated he would kill Duncan, he was a man; if he would do it, he would be even more a man. Only at one point does Macbeth answer this. He dares to do everything that becomes a man, he says, and who dares to do more is none. However, his objections are swept away by her passionate courage, which drives him to say admiringly that she should bear only male children.

When Macbeth urges the ruined gentlemen to take revenge against their supposed destroyer, Banquo, he makes a similar appeal to their manhood. Are they so "gospelled," he asks, that they will pray for the man who has ruined them? The teaching of the Gospels to love one's enemies is treated by him contemptuously. A real man, who is not a milksop, will respond to injuries by taking a bloody revenge.

When Macbeth sees the ghost of Banquo and betrays himself to his guests, Lady Macbeth makes use of her previous taunt to rouse him to himself. "Are you a man?" she asks. He is a man who will face a natural danger as bravely as any other, he answers, but this supernatural visit must affright anyone. Lady Macbeth treats the ghost as an hallucination and derides belief in it as a womanish credulity that credits old wives' tales. By the end of the scene Macbeth has accepted her view. He will go on, he says, until he becomes mature, a man, in crime.

The irony is that in doing so he becomes devoid of feeling so that when he hears of his wife's death he dismisses it with the observation that she had to die some time or other and it does not matter when, life being meaningless and futile. This contrasts with the way in which Macduff receives the news of the death of his wife and children. He is overcome with grief, and when Malcolm urges him to bear it as a man, he answers that he must also feel it as a man. The tender feelings are as much a part of manhood as anger and courage. Macduff has both, and he tempers his grief to avenge his family on the field of battle as God's agent.

RESEARCH AREAS

The Tragic Elements of Macbeth

The student may wish to write an essay of critical interpretation on one of the aspects of the tragedy, expanding upon or taking issue with a point made in this study guide or presenting some point not made here. He should in doing so read what other critics have had to say. No one would expect such a paper to be startlingly original. However, the student should assimilate his reading so that it has become a part of him and so that he applies whatever insights he has gained from it to his own reading of the play. Any indebtedness should, of course, be duly acknowledged. Critics should not be chosen at random. The BIBLIOGRAPHY, below, is one guide to criticism.

Critics of Macbeth*: Their Similarities and Differences*

Another kind of paper might compare what three or four critics dealing with similar concerns have had to say. Such a paper should do more than summarize the position of each critic. It should make an analytical comparison, showing points of agreement and disagreement and the contribution of each critic. Although *Macbeth* criticism does not have the same kind and number of great central issues that criticism of *Hamlet, Othello,* and *King Lear* has, the student will find many interesting controversies. For instance, if he wishes to read radically different interpretations of Macbeth's character than the Bradleyan one here presented, he may go to L. L. Shücking, Lily B. Campbell, E. E. Stoll (*Review of English Studies*, 1943; *From Shakespeare to Joyce,* 1944), and A. P. Rossiter (*Angel with Horns,* 1961).

Changing Critical Climates

Another kind of paper might compare what a number of critics of different historical periods have had to say about the play generally or about a specific element of the play. The porter's scene, for instance, has afforded a wide variety of interesting comments. The romantic critic Coleridge dismissed it as un-Shakespearean. His fellow romantic De Quincey wrote a celebrated essay on the knocking on the gate without mentioning the porter. The great Shakespeare scholar G. L. Kittredge sharply attacked Coleridge (*Shakespeare*, 1916). Other twentieth-century scholars who have written on the porter scene, to continue the example, are John W. Spargo (*J. Q. Adams Memorial Studies,* 1948), who takes issue with De Quincey; John B. Harcourt (*Shakespeare Quarterly,* 1961); Kenneth Muir ("New Arden" edition of *Macbeth*); and Glynne Wickham (*Shakespeare Survey,* 1966).

Macbeth *and Opposing Critical Approaches*

Still another kind of paper might compare what twentieth-century critics with different critical approaches have contributed to an understanding of the play—say, the character analysis of A. C. Bradley, the study of imagery of Caroline Spurgeon, the study of symbolism of G. Wilson Knight, the study of background intellectual history of E. M. W. Tillyard. A famous attack on Bradley's method is L. C. Knights's satirically titled essay, "How Many Children Had Lady Macbeth?" It presents as an alternative a study of the interplay of themes. An answer to it is Paul N. Siegel's "In Defense of Bradley" (*College English,* 1948). Cleanth Brooks's "The Naked Babe and the Cloak of Manliness" is a well-known essay, whose method of criticism, focussing on imagery and symbolism, was attacked by the distinguished critic Helen Gardner in *The Business of Criticism* (1959).

Backgrounds for an Understanding of Macbeth

Finally, the student may want to write a paper summarizing and synthesizing the results of research in a background area such as witchcraft in Elizabethan thought, the Elizabethan concept of the tyrant, or the Gunpowder Plot trial. He will find that scholars as well as critics disagree with each other, add to each other, and contribute in different ways to an understanding of the play. Volume XIX of *Shakespeare Survey* (1966) gives an excellent review of the work done in these and other fields.

MACBETH

DRAMATIS PERSONAE

DUNCAN, *king of Scotland.*

MALCOLM, DONALBAIN, } *his sons.*

MACBETH, BANQUO, } *generals of the king's army.*

MACDUFF, LENNOX, ROSS, MENTEITH, ANGUS, CAITHNESS, } *noblemen of Scotland.*

FLEANCE, *son to Banquo.*

SIWARD, *Earl of Northumberland, general of the English forces.*

YOUNG SIWARD, *his son.*

SEYTON, *an officer attending on Macbeth.*

BOY, *son to Macduff.*

An ENGLISH DOCTOR.

A SCOTCH DOCTOR.

A SOLDIER.

A PORTER.

An OLD MAN.

LADY MACBETH.

LADY MACDUFF.

GENTLEWOMAN *attending on Lady Macbeth.*

HECATE.

Three WITCHES.

APPARITIONS.

LORDS, GENTLEMAN, OFFICERS, SOLDIERS, MURDERERS, ATTENDANTS, *and* MESSENGERS.

SCENE: *Scotland: England.*

ACT I

SCENE I. *A desert place.*

[*Thunder and lightning. Enter three* WITCHES.]

FIRST WITCH. When shall we three meet again
In thunder, lightning, or in rain?
SEC. WITCH. When the hurlyburly's done,
When the battle's lost and won.
THIRD WITCH. That will be ere the set of sun.
FIRST WITCH. Where the place?
SEC. WITCH. Upon the heath.
THIRD WITCH. There to meet with Macbeth.
FIRST WITCH. I come, Graymalkin!
SEC. WITCH. Paddock calls.
THIRD WITCH. Anon.
ALL. Fair is foul, and foul is fair:
Hover through the fog and filthy air.

[*Exeunt.*

SCENE II. *A camp near Forres.*

[*Alarum within. Enter* DUNCAN, MALCOLM, DONALBAIN, LENNOX, *with* ATTENDANTS, *meeting a bleeding* SERGEANT.]

DUN. What bloody man is that? He can report,
As seemeth by his plight, of the revolt
The newest state.
MAL. This is the sergeant
Who like a good and hardy soldier fought
'Gainst my captivity. Hail, brave friend!
Say to the king the knowledge of the broil

Act I. Scene i: s.d. Alarum within, trumpet call to arms, offstage. **3. hurlyburly's** uproar's. **8. Graymalkin,** gray cat; one of the familiar spirits of the witch. **9. Paddock,** toad. **10. anon,** at once; i.e., I am coming at once. **Scene ii: 3. sergeant,** Captain of the King's guard. **5. 'Gainst my captivity,** to prevent my capture. **6. broil,** battle.

As thou didst leave it.
SER. Doubtful it stood;
As two spent swimmers, that do cling together
And choke their art. The merciless Macdonwald—
Worthy to be a rebel, for to that
The multiplying villanies of nature
Do swarm upon him—from the western isles
Of kerns and gallowglasses is supplied;
And fortune, on his damnèd quarrel smiling,
Show'd like a rebel's whore: but all's too weak:
For brave Macbeth—well he deserves that name—
Disdaining fortune, with his brandish'd steel,
Which smoked with bloody execution,
Like valour's minion carvèd out his passage
Till he faced the slave;
Which ne'er shook hands, nor bade farewell to him,
Till he unseam'd him from the nave to the chaps,
And fix'd his head upon our battlements.
DUN. O valiant cousin! worthy gentleman!
SER. As whence the sun 'gins his reflection
Shipwrecking storms and direful thunders break,
So from that spring whence comfort seem'd to come
Discomfort swells. Mark, king of Scotland, mark:
No sooner justice had with valour arm'd
Compell'd these skipping kerns to trust their heels,
But the Norweyan lord surveying vantage,
With furbish'd arms and new supplies of men
Began a fresh assault.
DUN. Dismay'd not this
Our captains, Macbeth and Banquo?

9. choke, render useless. **10. to that,** to accomplish that result (of making him a rebel). **13. Of . . . supplied,** has recruited an army of kerns (light-armed Gaelic foot-soldiers) and gallowglasses (Gaelic soldiers armed with axes who fought on horseback), both from the Hebrides. **15. Show'd . . . whore,** i.e., showed herself faithless to the rebel. **19. minion,** favorite. **21. which,** Macbeth. **22. nave,** navel; **chaps,** jaws. **25. whence,** i.e., in the east. **30. skipping,** leaping (in retreat). **31. surveying vantage,** seeing his opportunity. **32. furbish'd,** freshly

SER. Yes;
As sparrows eagles, or the hare the lion.
If I say sooth, I must report they were
As cannons overcharged with double cracks, so they
Doubly redoubled strokes upon the foe:
Except they meant to bathe in reeking wounds,
Or memorize another Golgotha,
I cannot tell.
But I am faint, my gashes cry for help.
DUN. So well thy words become thee as thy wounds;
They smack of honour both. Go get him surgeons.
[*Exit* SERGEANT, *attended.*]
Who comes here?

[*Enter* ROSS.]

MAL. The worthy thane of Ross.
LEN. What a haste looks through his eyes! So should he look
That seems to speak things strange.
ROSS. God save the king.
DUN. Whence camest thou, worthy thane?
ROSS. From Fife, great king;
Where the Norweyan banners flout the sky
And fan our people cold. Norway himself,
With terrible numbers,
Assisted by that most disloyal traitor
The thane of Cawdor, began a dismal conflict;
Till that Bellona's bridegroom, lapp'd in proof,
Confronted him with self-comparisons,
Point against point rebellious, arm 'gainst arm,
Curbing his lavish spirit: and, to conclude,

scoured. 37. **cracks,** charges. 40. **memorize,** make memorable; **Golgotha,** "place of the skull," where Jesus was crucified. 45. **thane,** a Scottish earl. 47. **seems,** seems about. 49. **flout,** insult. 50. **Norway himself,** the King of Norway. 54. **Bellona,** the Roman goddess of war; **lapp'd in proof,** clad in well-tested armor. 55. **Confronted . . . comparisons,** matched him stroke for stroke. 57. **lavish,** insolent.

The victory fell on us.
DUN. Great happiness!
ROSS. That now
Sweno, the Norway's king, craves composition;
Nor would we deign him burial of his men
Till he disbursèd at Saint Colme's inch
Ten thousand dollars to our general use.
DUN. No more that thane of Cawdor shall deceive
Our bosom interest: go pronounce his present death,
And with his former title greet Macbeth.
ROSS. I'll see it done.
DUN. What he hath lost noble Macbeth hath won. [*Exeunt.*

SCENE III. *A heath near Forres.*

[*Thunder. Enter the three* WITCHES.]

FIRST WITCH. Where hast thou been, sister?
SEC. WITCH. Killing swine.
THIRD WITCH. Sister, where thou?
FIRST WITCH. A sailor's wife had chestnuts in her lap,
And munch'd, and munch'd, and munch'd:—"Give me," quoth I:
"Aroint thee, witch!" the rump-fed ronyon cries.
Her husband's to Aleppo gone, master o' the Tiger:
But in a sieve I'll thither sail,
And, like a rat without a tail,
I'll do, I'll do, and I'll do.
SEC. WITCH. I'll give thee a wind.
FIRST WITCH. Thou'rt kind.
THIRD WITCH. And I another.
FIRST WITCH. I myself have all the other,

58. that, with the result that. **59. craves composition,** asks for terms of peace. **61. Saint Colme's inch,** Inchcolm, the small island of St. Colombia in the Firth of Forth near Edinburgh. **62. general,** public. **64. bosom interest,** matters of vital importance; **present,** immediate. **Scene iii: 6. Aroint,** begone; **rump-fed ronyon,** fat-rumped, scabby creature. **7. Tiger,** name of a ship. **9. rat . . . tail,** a witch transformed into an animal could be detected by a physical defect.

And the very ports they blow,
All the quarters that they know
I' the shipman's card.
I will drain him dry as hay:
Sleep shall neither night nor day
Hang upon his pent-house lid;
He shall live a man forbid:
Weary se'nnights nine times nine
Shall he dwindle, peak and pine:
Though his bark cannot be lost,
Yet it shall be tempest-tost.
Look what I have.

SEC. WITCH. Show me, show me.

FIRST WITCH. Here I have a pilot's thumb,
Wreck'd as homeward he did come.

[*Drum within.*

THIRD WITCH. A drum, a drum!
Macbeth doth come.

ALL. The weird sisters, hand in hand,
Posters of the sea and land,
Thus do go about, about:
Thrice to thine and thrice to mine
And thrice again, to make up nine.
Peace! the charm's wound up.

[*Enter* MACBETH *and* BANQUO.]

MACB. So foul and fair a day I have not seen.

BAN. How far is 't call'd to Forres? What are these
So wither'd and so wild in their attire,
That look not like the inhabitants o' the earth,
And yet are on 't? Live you? or are you aught
That man may question? You seem to understand me,

14. other, ie., others. **15. blow,** blow upon. **17. card,** compass. **20. pent-house lid,** eyelids sloping like the roof of a lean-to. **21. forbid,** accursed. **22. se'nnights,** weeks. **32. weird sisters,** sisters of destiny, i.e., the Fates. **33. Posters of,** swift travelers over. **35-6. Thrice . . . nine,** i.e., three times for each of the three sisters. **38. foul,** rainy, stormy.

By each at once her choppy finger laying
Upon her skinny lips: you should be women,
And yet your beards forbid me to interpret
That you are so.

MACB. Speak if you can: what are you?

FIRST WITCH. All hail, Macbeth! hail to thee, thane of Glamis!

SEC. WITCH. All hail, Macbeth! hail to thee, thane of Cawdor!

THIRD WITCH. All hail, Macbeth, that shalt be king hereafter!

BAN. Good sir, why do you start, and seem to fear
Things that do sound so fair? I' the name of truth,
Are ye fantastical, or that indeed
Which outwardly ye show? My noble partner
You greet with present grace and great prediction
Of noble having and of royal hope,
That he seems rapt withal: to me you speak not.
If you can look into the seeds of time,
And say which grain will grow and which will not,
Speak then to me, who neither beg nor fear
Your favours nor your hate.

FIRST WITCH. Hail!

SEC. WITCH. Hail!

THIRD WITCH. Hail!

FIRST WITCH. Lesser than Macbeth, and greater.

SEC. WITCH. Not so happy, yet much happier.

THIRD WITCH. Thou shalt get kings, though thou be none:
So all hail, Macbeth and Banquo!

FIRST WITCH. Banquo and Macbeth, all hail!

MACB. Stay, you imperfect speakers, tell me more:
By Sinel's death I know I am thane of Glamis;

44. choppy, chapped. **53. fantastical,** creatures of the imagination. **54. show,** appear to be. **55-6. with . . . royal hope,** with his present title of nobility and with prophecy of great noble and royal estate. **57. rapt withal,** carried out of himself by it. **67. get,** beget. **70. imperfect,** incomplete (as regards information).

But how of Cawdor? the thane of Cawdor lives,
A prosperous gentleman; and to be king
Stands not within the prospect of belief,
No more than to be Cawdor. Say from whence
You owe this strange intelligence? or why
Upon this blasted heath you stop our way
With such prophetic greeting? Speak, I charge you.
[WITCHES *vanish.*

BAN. The earth hath bubbles, as the water has,
And these are of them. Whither are they vanish'd?

MACB. Into the air; and what seem'd corporal melted
As breath into the wind. Would they had stay'd!

BAN. Were such things here as we do speak about?
Or have we eaten on the insane root
That takes the reason prisoner?

MACB. Your children shall be kings.

BAN. You shall be king.

MACB. And thane of Cawdor too: went it not so?

BAN. To the selfsame tune and words. Who's here?

[*Enter* ROSS *and* ANGUS.]

ROSS. The king hath happily received, Macbeth,
The news of thy success; and when he reads
Thy personal venture in the rebels' fight,
His wonders and his praises do contend
Which should be thine or his: silenced with that,
In viewing o'er the rest o' the selfsame day,
He finds thee in the stout Norweyan ranks,
Nothing afeard of what thyself didst make,
Strange images of death. As thick as hail
Came post with post; and every one did bear
Thy praises in his kingdom's great defence,
And pour'd them down before him.

71. **Sinel,** Macbeth's father. 76. **owe,** have; **intelligence,** information. 84. **insane root,** a root supposed to cause insanity, perhaps hemlock. 92-3. **His wonders . . . with that,** the King is silenced, being torn between the impulse to express his own wonder and his desire to praise

ANG. We are sent
To give thee from our royal master thanks;
Only to herald thee into his sight,
Not pay thee.
ROSS. And, for an earnest of a greater honour,
He bade me, from him, call thee thane of Cawdor:
In which addition, hail, most worthy thane!
For it is thine.
BAN. What, can the devil speak true?
MACB. The thane of Cawdor lives: why do you dress me
In borrow'd robes?
ANG. Who was the thane lives yet;
But under heavy judgement bears that life
Which he deserves to lose. Whether he was combined
With those of Norway, or did line the rebel
With hidden help and vantage, or that with both
He labour'd in his country's wreck, I know not;
But treasons capital, confess'd and proved,
Have overthrown him.
MACB. [*Aside*] Glamis, and thane of Cawdor!
The greatest is behind. [*To* ROSS *and* ANGUS]
Thanks for your pains.
[*To* BAN.] Do you not hope your children shall be kings,
When those that gave the thane of Cawdor to me
Promised no less to them?
BAN. That trusted home
Might yet enkindle you unto the crown,
Besides the thane of Cawdor. But 'tis strange:
And oftentimes, to win us to our harm,
The instruments of darkness tell us truths,

Macbeth. **97. Strange images,** horrible forms. **98. post with post,** one hurrying messenger after another. **99. his, i.e., the** King's. **102. herald thee,** conduct thee solemnly. **104. earnest,** pledge. **106. addition,** title. **110. judgement,** sentence. **121. those of Norway,** the Norwegian forces; **line,** aid. 113. **help and vantage,** help for his advantage; **with both,** i.e., Macdonwald and the King of Norway. **114. wreck,** ruin. **115. capital,** for which death is the penalty. **120. That . . . home,** if that were fully believed.

Win us with honest trifles, to betray's
In deepest consequence.
Cousins, a word, I pray you.
MACB. [*Aside*] Two truths are told,
As happy prologues to the swelling act
Of the imperial theme.—I thank you, gentlemen.
[*Aside*] This supernatural soliciting
Cannot be ill, cannot be good: if ill,
Why hath it given me earnest of success,
Commencing in a truth? I am thane of Cawdor:
If good, why do I yield to that suggestion
Whose horrid image doth unfix my hair
And make my seated heart knock at my ribs,
Against the use of nature? Present fears
Are less than horrible imaginings:
My thought, whose murder yet is but fantastical,
Shakes so my single state of man that function
Is smother'd in surmise, and nothing is
But what is not.
BAN. Look, how our partner's rapt.
MACB. [*Aside*] If chance will have me king, why, chance may crown me,
Without my stir.
BAN. New honours come upon him,
Like our strange garments, cleave not to their mould
But with the aid of use.
MACB. [*Aside*] Come what come may,
Time and the hour runs through the roughest day.
BAN. Worthy Macbeth, we stay upon your leisure.
MACB. Give me your favour: my dull brain was wrought

126. In . . . consequence, in matters of great importance to follow. **128. swelling,** magnificent. **130. soliciting,** temptation (of the witches). **131. ill,** of evil origin. **136. seated,** firm. **137. Against . . . nature,** contrary to ordinary experience. **139. murder . . . fantastical,** idea of murder is only a suggestion of my imagination. **140. single . . . man,** unified kingdom of my being, i.e., my microcosm. **140-1. function . . . surmise,** my normal course of thought and action is overwhelmed by my imaginings. **144. my stir,** action on my part. **145. strange,** new;

With things forgotten. Kind gentlemen, your pains
Are register'd where every day I turn
The leaf to read them. Let us toward the king.
Think upon what hath chanced, and, at more time,
The interim having weigh'd it, let us speak
Our free hearts each to other.
BAN. Very gladly.
MACB. Till then, enough. Come, friends.
[*Exeunt.*

SCENE IV. *Forres. The palace.*

[*Flourish. Enter* DUNCAN, MALCOLM, DONALBAIN, LENNOX, *and* ATTENDANTS.]

DUN. Is execution done on Cawdor? Are not
Those in commission yet return'd?
MAL. My liege,
They are not yet come back. But I have spoke
With one that saw him die: who did report
That very frankly he confess'd his treasons,
Implor'd your highness' pardon and set forth
A deep repentance: nothing in his life
Became him like the leaving it; he died
As one that had been studied in his death
To throw away the dearest thing he owed,
As 'twere a careless trifle.
DUN. There's no art
To find the mind's construction in the face:
He was a gentleman on whom I built
An absolute trust.

cleave . . . mould, i.e., do not fit. **149. favour,** pardon; **wrought,** agitated. **150. things forgotten,** i.e., things I am trying to remember. **151-2. where . . . read them,** i.e., in my memory. **154. interim . . . weigh'd it,** having considered it in the meantime. **155. Our free hearts,** our hearts freely. **Scene iv: s.d. flourish,** fanfare played by the trumpets. **2. Those in commission,** those commissioned to execute (Cawdor). **9. studied in his death,** i.e., had learned the role of effective (indifferent) dying. **10. owed,** owned. **11. careless,** worthless.

[*Enter* MACBETH, BANQUO, ROSS, *and* ANGUS.]

O worthiest cousin!
The sin of my ingratitude even now
Was heavy on me: thou art so far before
That swiftest wing of recompense is slow
To overtake thee. Would thou hadst less deserved,
That the proportion both of thanks and payment
Might have been mine! only I have left to say,
More is thy due than more than all can pay.

MACB. The service and the loyalty I owe,
In doing it, pays itself. Your highness' part
Is to receive our duties; and our duties
Are to your throne and state children and servants,
Which do but what they should, by doing every thing
Safe toward your love and honour.

DUN. Welcome hither:
I have begun to plant thee, and will labour
To make thee full of growing. Noble Banquo,
That hast no less deserved, nor must be known
No less to have done so, let me infold thee
And hold thee to my heart.

BAN. There if I grow,
The harvest is your own.

DUN. My plenteous joys,
Wanton in fulness, seek to hide themselves
In drops of sorrow. Sons, kinsmen, thanes,
And you whose places are the nearest, know
We will establish our estate upon
Our eldest, Malcolm, whom we name hereafter
The Prince of Cumberland; which honour must

12. mind's construction, interpretation of the mind. **15. of my ingratitude,** of being unable to express my gratitude sufficiently. **19-20. That . . . been mine,** i.e., that it might have been in my power to reward you in proportion (to your deserts). **27. Safe toward,** toward making secure. **28. to plant thee,** i.e., by making you thane of Cawdor. **34. wanton,** unrestrained. **36 nearest,** closest in my regard. **37. establish**

Not unaccompanied invest him only,
But signs of nobleness, like stars, shall shine
On all deservers. From hence to Inverness,
And bind us further to you.

MACB. The rest of labour, which is not used for you
I'll be myself the harbinger and make joyful
The hearing of my wife with your approach;
So humbly take my leave.

DUN. My worthy Cawdor!

MACB. [*Aside*] *The Prince of Cumberland! that is a step*
On which I must fall down, or else o'er leap,
For in my way it lies. Stars, hide your fires;
Let not light see my black and deep desires:
The eye wink at the hand; yet let that be,
Which the eye fears, when it is done, to see

[*Exit.*

DUN. True, worthy Banquo; he is full so valiant,
And in his commendations I am fed;
It is a banquet to me. Let's after him,
Whose care is gone before to bid us welcome:
It is a peerless kinsman. [*Flourish. Exeunt.*

SCENE V. *Inverness.* MACBETH'S *castle.*

[*Enter* LADY MACBETH, *reading a letter.*]

LADY M. "They met me in the day of success; and I have learned by the perfectest report, they have more in them than mortal knowledge. When I burned in desire to question them further, they made themselves air, into which they vanished. Whiles I stood rapt in the wonder of it, came missives from the king, who all-hailed

our estate, fix the succession of our kingship. **39. Prince of Cumberland,** title bestowed on the heir to the throne. **43. bind us further,** i.e., by being our host. **44. used for you,** devoted to serving you. **45. harbinger,** messenger sent ahead of the King to arrange suitable lodgings. **52. eye . . . hand,** let the eyes be closed to what the hand does. **54 full so valiant,** just as valiant as you say he is. **Scene v: 7. missives,** messengers. **10-1. referred . . . time,** made me a promise me 'Thane of Cawdor'; by which title, before, these weird sisters saluted me, and referred me to the coming on of time, with 'Hail, king that shalt be!' This have I thought good to deliver thee, my dearest partner of greatness, that thou mightst not lose the dues of rejoicing, by being ignorant of what greatness is promised thee. Lay it to they heart, and farewell."

Glamis thou art, and Cawdor; and shalt be
What thou art promised: yet do I fear thy nature;
It is too full o' the milk of human kindness
To catch the nearest way: thou wouldst be great;
Art not without ambition, but without
The illness should attend it: what thou wouldst highly,
That wouldst thou holily; wouldst not play false,
And yet wouldst wrongly win: thou 'ldst have, great Glamis,
That which cries "Thus thou must do, if thou have it;
And that which rather thou dost fear to do
Than wishest should be undone." Hie thee hither,
That I may pour my spirits in thine ear;
And chastise with the valour of my tongue
All that impedes thee from the golden round,
Which fate and metaphysical aid doth seem
To have thee crown'd withal.

[*Enter a* MESSENGER.]

What is your tidings?

MESS. The king comes here to-night.

LADY M. Thou'rt mad to say it:
Is not thy master with him? who, were 't so,
Would have inform'd for preparation.

MESS. So please you, it is true: our thane is coming
One of my fellows had the speed of him,

for the future. **18. milk . . . kindness,** gentleness of human nature. **19. catch . . . way,** adopt the most direct course. **21. illness,** evil nature. **26. Hie thee,** hurry. **28. valour . . . tongue,** i.e., with the bold things I shall say. **29. golden round,** crown. **30. metaphysical,** supernatural. **34. for preparation,** in time to make preparations.

Who, almost dead for breath, had scarcely more
Than would make up his message.
LADY M. Give him tending;
He brings great news. [*Exit* MESSENGER.]
The raven himself is hoarse
That croaks the fatal entrance of Duncan
Under my battlements. Come, you spirits
That tend on mortal thoughts, unsex me here,
And fill me from the crown to the toe top-full
Of direst cruelty! make thick my blood;
Stop up the access and passage to remorse,
That no compunctious vistings of nature
Shake my fell purpose, nor keep peace between
The effect and it! Come to my woman's breasts,
And take my milk for gall, you murdering ministers,
Wherever in your sightless substances
You wait on nature's mischief! Come, thick night,
And pall thee in the dunnest smoke of hell,
That my keen knife see not the wound it makes,
Nor heaven peep through the blanket of the dark,
To cry "Hold, hold!"

[*Enter* MACBETH.]

Great Glamis! worthy Cawdor!
Greater than both, by the all-hail hereafter!
Thy letters have transported me beyond
This ignorant present, and I feel now
The future in the instant.
MACB. My dearest love,
Duncan comes here to-night.

36. **had . . . him,** outran him. 42. **tend . . . thoughts,** foster thoughts of murder. 44. **thick,** thin blood was supposed to indicate cowardice. 46. **compunctious . . . nature,** instinctive feelings of pity. 47. **fell,** cruel. 47-8. **keep . . . and it,** i.e., hinder my purpose from fulfillment. 49. **murdering ministers,** instruments of murder (the evil spirits she has invoked). 50. **sightless,** invisible. 51. **wait . . . mischief,** serve evil in the world. 52. **pall,** wrap; **dunnest,** blackest. 56. **all-hail hereafter,** the future which I now salute. 59. **The future . . . instant,**

LADY M. And when goes hence?
MACB. To-morrow, as he purposes.
LADY M. O, never
Shall sun that morrow see!
Your face, my thane, is as a book where men
May read strange matters. To beguile the time,
Look like the time; bear welcome in your eye,
Your hand, your tongue: look like the innocent flower,
But be the serpent under 't. He that's coming
Must be provided for: and you shall put
This night's great business into my dispatch;
Which shall to all our nights and days to come
Give solely sovereign sway and masterdom.
MACB. We will speak further.
LADY M. Only look up clear;
To alter favour ever is to fear:
Leave all the rest to me. [*Exeunt.*

SCENE VI. *Before* MACBETH'S *castle.*

[*Hautboys and torches. Enter* DUNCAN, MALCOLM, DONALBAIN, BANQUO, LENNOX, MACDUFF, ROSS, ANGUS, *and* ATTENDANTS.]

DUN. This castle hath a pleasant seat; the air
Nimbly and sweetly recommends itself
Unto our gentle senses.
BAN. This guest of summer,
The temple-haunting martlet, does approve,
By his loved mansionry, that the heaven's breath

i.e., you seem already to be king. **65. Look like the time,** assume the bearing the occasion demands. **60. dispatch,** management. **71. Give solely,** i.e., the only thing that will give. **72. look up clear,** keep your face unclouded. **73. favour,** facial expression; **to fear,** i.e., to betray yourself. **Scene vi: s.d. Hautboys,** oboes. **1. seat,** situation. **2. Nimbly,** briskly. **gentle,** soothed. **4. temple-haunting martlet,** the martin (a small swallow) which often built its nest in church towers; **approve,** demonstrate. **5. By . . . mansionry,** by the fact that he chose this as a loved site for his home (nest). **6. jutty,** projection. **7. coign of vantage,** convenient nook.

Smells wooingly here: no jutty, frieze,
Buttress, nor coign of vantage, but this bird
Hath made his pendent bed and procreant cradle:
Where they most breed and haunt, I have observed,
The air is delicate.

[*Enter* LADY MACBETH.]

DUN. See, see, our honour'd hostess!
The love that follows us sometime is our trouble,
Which still we thank as love. Herein I teach you
How you shall bid God 'ild us for your pains,
And thank us for your trouble.
LADY M. All our service
In every point twice done and then done double
Were poor and single business to contend
Against those honours deep and broad wherewith
Your majesty loads our house: for those of old,
And the late dignities heap'd up to them,
We rest your hermits.
DUN. Where's the thane of Cawdor?
We coursed him at the heels, and had a purpose
To be his purveyor: but he rides well;
And his great love, sharp as his spur, hath holp him
To his home before us. Fair and noble hostess,
We are your guest to-night.
LADY M. Your servants ever
Have theirs, themselves and what is theirs, in compt,
To make their audit at your highness' pleasure,
Still to return your own.

8. **procreant cradle,** breeding place. 10. **delicate,** agreeable. 11-2. **The love . . . love,** the love which attends me is sometimes an inconvenience, but I am nevertheless grateful for it because it is love. 12. **Herein,** i.e., by this speech. 13. **'ild,** for "yield," reward. 14. **your trouble,** the inconvenience to which I have put you. 16-7. **Were . . . Against,** would be of little weight in comparison with. 18. **those of old,** past honors. 19. **late,** recent. 20. **rest . . . hermits,** remain your beadsmen who continue to pray (tell our beads) for you. 21. **coursed,** pursued. 22. **purveyor,** an officer sent ahead of the king to arrange his lodging, here = forerunner. 26. **in compt,** on deposit. 27. **make . . .**

DUN. Give me your hand;
Conduct me to mine host: we love him highly,
And shall continue our graces towards him.
By your leave, hostess.

[*Exeunt.*

SCENE VII. MACBETH'S *castle.*

[*Hautboys and torches. Enter a* SEWER, *and divers* SERVANTS *with dishes and service, and pass over the stage. Then enter* MACBETH.]

MACB. If it were done when 'tis done, then 'twere well
It were done quickly: if the assassination
Could trammel up the consequence, and catch
With his surcease success; that but this blow
Might be the be-all and end-all here,
But here, upon this bank and shoal of time,
We'ld jump the life to come. But in these cases
We still have judgement here; that we but teach
Bloody instructions, which, being taught, return
To plague the inventor: this even-handed justice
Commends the ingredients of our poison'd chalice
To our own lips. He's here in double trust;
First, as I am his kinsman and his subject,
Strong both against the deed; then, as his host,
Who should against his murderer shut the door,
Not bear the knife myself. Besides, this Duncan
Hath borne his faculties so meek, hath been
So clear in his great office, that his virtues
Will plead like angels, trumpet-tongued, against

audit, render you an account. **28. Still,** i.e., at any moment; **your own,** what they owe you, i.e., duty. **30. graces,** favors. **31. By your leave,** i.e., with your permission I will retire; a courteous formula of leave-taking. **Scene vii: s.d., Sewer,** butler. **3. trammel up,** catch, as in a net. **4. his surcease,** his cessation, Duncan's death; **that,** so that. **7. jump,** risk. **8. here,** in this world; **that,** with the result that. **14. Strong both,** both facts are strong arguments. **17. borne . . . so meek,**

The deep damnation of his taking-off;
And pity, like a naked new-born babe,
Striding the blast, or heaven's cherubim, horsed
Upon the sightless couriers of the air,
Shall blow the horrid deed in every eye,
That tears shall drown the wind. I have no spur
To prick the sides of my intent, but only
Vaulting ambition which o'erleaps itself
And falls on the other.

[*Enter* LADY MACBETH.]

How now! what news?

LADY M. He has almost supp'd: why have you left the chamber?

MACB. Hath he ask'd for me?

LADY M. Know you not he has?

MACB. We will proceed no further in this business:
He hath honour'd me of late; and I have bought
Golden opinions from all sorts of people,
Which would be worn now in their newest gloss,
Not cast aside so soon.

LADY M. Was the hope drunk
Wherein you dress'd yourself? hath it slept since?
And wakes it now, to look so green and pale
At what it did so freely? From this time
Such I account thy love. Art thou afeard
To be the same in thine own act and valour
As thou art in desire? Wouldst thou have that
Which thou esteem'st the ornament of life,
And live a coward in thine own esteem,
Letting "I dare not" wait upon "I would,"
Like the poor cat i' the adage?

exercised his royal authority so mildly. **18. clear,** unspotted. **23. sightless . . . air,** invisible horsemen of the air, the wind. **28. the other,** the other side. **29. chamber,** banqueting-hall. **34. would be,** demand to be. **37. green,** sick. **38. freely,** without compulsion.

MACB. Prithee, peace:
I dare do all that may become a man;
Who dares do more is none.
LADY M. What beast was 't, then,
That made you break this enterprise to me?
When you durst do it, then you were a man;
And, to be more than what you were, you would
Be so much more the man. Nor time nor place
Did then adhere, and yet you would make both:
They have made themselves, and that their fitness now
Does unmake you. I have given suck, and know
How tender 'tis to love the babe that milks me:
I would, while it was smiling in my face,
Have pluck'd my nipple from his boneless gums,
And dash'd the brains out, had I so sworn as you
Have done to this.
MACB. If we should fail?
LADY M. We fail!
But screw your courage to the sticking-place,
And we'll not fail. When Duncan is asleep—
Whereto the rather shall his day's hard journey
Soundly invite him—his two chamberlains
Will I with wine and wassail so convince
That memory, the warder of the brain,
Shall be a fume, and the receipt of reason
A limebeck only; when in swinish sleep
Their drenched natures lie as in a death,
What cannot you and I perform upon
The unguarded Duncan? what not put upon

45. **adage,** "The cat would eat fish and would not wet her feet." 48. **break,** broach. 52. **Did then adhere,** were then suitable. 54. **unmake,** unman. 57. **boneless,** toothless. 58. **sworn,** been forsworn. 62. **rather,** earlier. 63. **chamberlains,** officers of the King's bedchamber. 64. **wassail,** wine to which spices and other ingredients are added; **convince,** overpower. 67. **limbeck,** for alembic, an apparatus used in distillation, a still. 65-7. **That memory . . . limbeck only,** i.e., as in a still the fumes of wine will rise from the stomach to the base of the brain, the supposed seat of memory, and thence to the receptacle (receipt) of reason, supposedly situated at the top

His spongy officers, who shall bear the guilt
Of our great quell?
MACB. Bring forth men-children only;
For thy undaunted mettle should compose
Nothing but males. Will it not be received,
When we have mark'd with blood those sleepy two
Of his own chamber and used their very daggers,
That they have done 't?
LADY M. Who dares receive it other,
As we shall make our griefs and clamour roar
Upon his death?
MACB. I am settled, and bend up
Each corporal agent to this terrible feat.
Away, and mock the time with fairest show:
False face must hide what the false heart doth know.
[*Exeunt.*

ACT II

SCENE I. *Court of* MACBETH'S *castle.*

[*Enter* BANQUO, *and* FLEANCE *bearing a torch before him.*]

BAN. How goes the night, boy?
FLE. The moon is down; I have not heard the clock.
BAN. And she goes down at twelve.
FLE. I take 't, 'tis later, sir.
BAN. Hold, take my sword. There's husbandry in heaven;
Their candles are all out. Take thee that too.
A heavy summons lies like lead upon me,
And yet I would not sleep: merciful powers,
Restrain in me the cursed thoughts that nature
Gives way to in repose!

of the brain under the skull. Thus memory and then reason will be blotted out. **71. spongy,** soaked, drunken. **72. quell,** murder. **74. received,** believed. **77. other,** otherwise. **79. I am settled,** my mind is made up; **bend up,** stretch taut, as a bow. **80. corporal agent to,** bodily faculty ready for. **81. mock the time,** deceive everyone. **Act II, Scene i: 4. husbandry,** economy. **5. that,** i.e., his dagger.

[*Enter* MACBETH, *and a* SERVANT *with a torch.*]

Give me my sword.
Who's there?

MACB. A friend.

BAN. What, sir, not yet at rest? The king's a-bed:
He hath been in unusual pleasure, and
Sent forth great largess to your offices.
This diamond he greets your wife withal,
By the name of most kind hostess; and shut up
In measureless content.

MACB. Being unprepared,
Our will became the servant to defect;
Which else should free have wrought.

BAN. All's well.
I dreamt last night of the three weird sisters:
To you they have show'd some truth.

MACB. I think not of them:
Yet, when we can entreat an hour to serve,
We would spend it in some words upon that business,
If you would grant the time.

BAN. At your kind'st leisure.

MACB. If you shall cleave to my consent, when 'tis,
It shall make honour for you.

BAN. So I lose none
In seeking to augment it, but still keep
My bosom franchised and allegiance clear,
I shall be counsell'd.

MACB. Good repose the while!

BAN. Thanks, sir: the like to you!

[*Exeunt* BANQUO *and* FLEANCE.

14. largess . . . offices, gifts of money to your servants' quarters. **16-17. shut . . . content,** he concluded the day in a state of complete satisfaction. **18. Our will . . . defect,** our desire (to entertain him properly) was hampered by our lack of preparation. **19. Which,** i.e., our will. **22. entreat . . . serve,** find time for the purpose. **25. cleave . . . consent,** adhere to my cause; **when 'tis,** i.e., when the proper time comes. **28. franchised,** free (from a sense of guilt); **clear,** spotless. **29. be**

MACB. Go bid thy mistress, when my drink is ready.
She strike upon the bell. Get thee to bed.
[*Exit* SERVANT.]
Is this a dagger which I see before me,
The handle toward my hand? Come, let me clutch thee.
I have thee not, and yet I see thee still.
Art thou not, fatal vision, sensible
To feeling as to sight? or art thou but
A dagger of the mind, a false creation,
Proceeding from the heat-oppressèd brain?
I see thee yet, in form as palpable
As this which now I draw.
Thou marshall'st me the way that I was going;
And such an instrument I was to use.
Mine eyes are made the fools o' the other senses,
Or else worth all the rest; I see thee still,
And on thy blade and dudgeon gouts of blood,
Which was not so before. There's no such thing:
It is the bloody business which informs
Thus to mine eyes. Now o'er the one half-world
Nature seems dead, and wicked dreams abuse
The curtain'd sleep; witchcraft celebrates
Pale Hecate's offerings, and wither'd murder,
Alarum'd by his sentinel, the wolf,
Whose howl's his watch, thus with his stealthy pace,
With Tarquin's ravishing strides, towards his design
Moves like a ghost. Thou sure and firm-set earth,
Hear not my steps, which way they walk, for fear
Thy very stones prate of my whereabout,
And take the present horror from the time,

counsell'd, follow your advice. **36. fatal,** sent by fate, hence prophetic; **sensible,** perceptible. **42. marshll'st,** leadest. **46. dungeon,** hilt; **gouts,** big drops. **48-9. informs Thus to,** creates this shape for. **50. abuse,** deceive. **51. curtain'd,** beds were enclosed by curtains. **52. Hecate,** classical goddess of the underworld, hence of witchcraft. **53. Alarum'd,** summoned to action. **54. Whose . . . watch,** i.e., the wolf's howl is like the striking of a clock, a signal for murder. **53. Tarquin,** an early Roman tyrant who ravised Lucretia.

Which now suits with it. Whiles I threat, he lives:
Words to the heat of deeds too cold breath gives.

[*A bell rings.*]

I go, and it is done; the bell invites me.
Hear it not, Duncan; for it is a knell
That summons thee to heaven or to hell.

[*Exit.*

SCENE II. *The same.*

[*Enter* LADY MACBETH.]

LADY M. That which hath made them drunk hath made me bold;
What hath quench'd them hath given me fire. Hark! Peace!
It was the owl that shriek'd, the fatal bellman,
Which gives the stern'st good-night. He is about it:
The doors are open; and the surfeited grooms
Do mock their charge with snores: I have drugg'd their possets,
That death and nature do contend about them,
Whether they live or die.

MACB. [*Within*] Who's there? what, ho!

LADY M. Alack, I am afraid they have awaked,
And 'tis not done. The attempt and not the deed
Confounds us. Hark! I laid their daggers ready;
He could not miss 'em. Had he not resembled
My father as he slept, I had done 't.

My husband!

MACB. I have done the deed. Didst thou not hear a noise?

59. And take . . . time, catch the feeling of horror appropriate to the silence of midnight (and so make my footsteps resound and betray me). **Scene ii: 3. fatal bellman,** the nightwatchman customarily visited condemned prisoners the night before their execution and rang a handbell outside their cell, urging them to repent of their sins. **5. surfeited grooms,** drunken servants of the chamber. **6. mock their charge,** make a mocking of guarding the King; **possets,** a kind of milk punch. **7. That,** so that; them, the grooms. **11. attempt,** i.e., a failed attempt. **12. Confounds,** will ruin.

[*Enter* MACBETH.]

LADY M. I heard the owl scream and the crickets cry.
Did not you speak?

MACB. When?

LADY M. Now.

MACB. As I descended?

LADY M. Ay.

MACB. Hark!
Who lies i' the second chamber?

LADY M. Donalbain.

MACB. This is a sorry sight.

[*Looking on his hands.*

LADY M. A foolish thought, to say a sorry sight.

MACB. There's one did laugh in 's sleep, and one cried "Murder!"
That they did wake each other: I stood and heard them:
But they did say their prayers, and address'd them
Again to sleep.

LADY M. There are two lodged together.

MACB. One cried "God bless us!" and "Amen" the other;
As they had seen me with these hangman's hands.
Listening their fear, I could not say "Amen,"
When they did say "God bless us!"

LADY M. Consider it not so deeply.

MACB. But wherefore could not I pronounce "Amen"?
I had most need of blessing, and "Amen"
Stuck in my throat.

LADY M. These deeds must not be thought
After these ways; so, it will make us mad.

MACB. Methought I heard a voice cry "Sleep no more!
Macbeth does murder sleep," the innocent sleep,
Sleep that knits up the ravell'd sleave of care,

21. sorry, grievous. **28. hangman's hands,** the executioner of men guilty of high treason was compelled to tear out the vitals of his victims with his bare hands. **29. fear,** the signs of their fear, their prayers. **34. so,** to do so. **37. knits . . . care,** binds up the skein (of consciousness) tangled by care.

The death of each day's life, sore labour's bath,
Balm of hurt minds, great nature's second course,
Chief nourisher in life's feast,—
LADY M. What do you mean?
MACB. Still it cried "Sleep no more!" to all the house:
"Glamis hath murder'd sleep, and therefore Cawdor
Shall sleep no more; Macbeth shall sleep no more."
LADY M. Who was it that thus cried? Why, worthy thane,
You do unbend your noble strength, to think
So brainsickly of things. Go get some water,
And wash this filthy witness from your hand.
Why did you bring these daggers from the place?
They must lie there: go carry them; and smear
The sleepy grooms with blood.
MACB. I'll go no more:
I am afraid to think what I have done;
Look on 't again I dare not.
LADY M. Infirm of purpose!
Give me the daggers: the sleeping and the dead
Are but as pictures: 'tis the eye of childhood
That fears a painted devil. If he do bleed,
I'll gild the faces of the grooms withal;
For it must seem their guilt.
[*Exit. Knocking within.*
MACB. Whence is that knocking?
How is 't with me, when every noise appals me?
What hands are here? ha! they pluck out mine eyes.
Will all great Neptune's ocean wash this blood
Clean from my hand? No, this my hand will rather
The multitudinous seas incarnadine,
Making the green one red.

39. second course, the second course was the most substantial part of an Elizabethan meal. **47. witness,** evidence. **54. pictures,** images (of living people). **55. bleed,** as a corpse was supposed to do in the presence of its murderer. **59. pluck . . . eyes,** make my eyes bulge.

[*Re-enter* LADY MACBETH.]

LADY M. My hands are of your colour; but I shame
To wear a heart so white. [*Knocking within.*] I hear a knocking
At the south entry: retire we to our chamber:
A little water clears us of this deed:
How easy is it, then! Your constancy
Hath left you unattended. [*Knocking within.*] Hark! More knocking.
Get on your nightgown, lest occasion call us,
And show us to be watchers. Be not lost
So poorly in your thoughts.

MACB. To know my deed, 'twere best not know myself.
[*Knocking within.*]
Wake Duncan with thy knocking! I would thou couldst!
[*Exeunt.*

SCENE III. *The same.*

[*Knocking within. Enter a* PORTER.]

PORTER. Here's a knocking indeed! If a man were porter of hell-gate, he should have old turning the key. [*Knocking within.*] Knock, knock, knock! Who's there, i' the name of Beelzebub? Here's a farmer, that hanged himself on the expectation of plenty: come in time; have napkins enow about you; here you'll sweat for 't. [*Knocking within.*] Knock, knock! Who's there, in the other devil's name? Faith,

62. incarnadine, make red. **63. one red,** one mass of red. **65. white,** i.e., bloodless and so cowardly. **68-9. constancy . . . unattended,** your self-command has deserted you. **70. nightgown,** dressing gown; occasion, this emergency. **71. watchers,** awake, i.e., not gone to bed. **72. So poorly,** in so poor-spirited a manner. **73. To know . . . myself,** i.e., if I am to face what I have done it will be better for me not to face myself. **Scene iii: 2. old,** a slang term for emphasis; cf. "a high old time." **4. Beelzebub,** the prince of devils. **4-5. farmer . . . plenty,** the farmer, a hoarder of grain, expecting to sell at top prices, foresaw a large harvest and subsequent low prices and ruin. **6. come in time,** a conventional phrase of welcome; **napkins enow,** handkerchiefs enough. **9-10. swear . . . scale,** swear to the truth of an ambiguous here's an equivocator, that could swear in both the scales against either scale; who committed treason enough for God's sake, yet could not equivocate to heaven: O, come in, equivocator. [*Knocking within.*] Knock, knock, knock! Who's there? Faith, here's an English tailor come hither, for stealing out of a French hose: come in, tailor; here you may roast your goose. [*Knocking within.*] Knock, knock; never at quiet! What are you? But this place is too cold for hell. I'll devil-porter it no further: I had thought to have let in some of all professions that go the primrose way to the everlasting bonfire. [*Knocking within.*] Anon, anon! I pray you, remember the porter. [*Opens the gate.*

[*Enter* MACDUFF *and* LENNOX.]

MACD. Was it so late, friend, ere you went to bed, That you do lie so late?

PORT. 'Faith, sir, we were carousing till the second cock: and drink, sir, is a great provoker of three things.

MACD. What three things does drink especially provoke?

PORT. Marry, sir, nose-painting, sleep, and urine. Lechery, sir, it provokes, and unprovokes; it provokes the desire, but it takes away the performance: therefore, much drink may be said to be an equivocator with lechery: it makes him, and it mars him; it sets him on, and it takes him off; it persuades him, and disheartens him; makes him stand to, and not stand to; in conclusion, equivocates him in a sleep, and, giving him the lie, leaves him.

MACD. I believe drink gave thee the lie last night.

PORT. That it did, sir, i' the very throat on me: but I requited him for his lie; and, I think, being too strong for him,

statement. **11. for God's sake,** i.e., for the sake of the Church. **12. equivocator,** one who makes ambiguous statements for the deliberate purpose of deceit. **15. French hose,** they were tight fitting; so only a practiced thief could steal any of their material. **16. goose,** a tailor's flatiron. **22. Anon.** in a minute. **27. second cock,** i.e., 3:00 A.M. **41. gave** though he took up my legs sometime, yet I made a shift to cast him.

MACD. Is thy master stirring?

[*Enter* MACBETH.]

Our knocking has awaked him; here he comes.
LEN. Good morrow, noble sir.
MACB. Good morrow, both.
MACD. Is the king stirring, worthy thane?
MACB. Not yet.
MACD. He did command me to call timely on him:
I have almost slipp'd the hour.
MACB. I know this is a joyful trouble to you;
But yet 'tis one.
MACB. The labour we delight in physics pain.
This is the door.
MACD. I'll make so bold to call,
For 'tis my limited service. [*Exit.*
LEN. Goes the king hence to-day?
MACB. He does: he did appoint so.
LEN. The night has been unruly: where we lay,
Our chimneys were blown down; and, as they say,
Lamenting heard i' the air; strange screams of death,
And prophesying with accents terrible
Of dire combuction and confused events
New hatch'd to the woeful time: the obscure bird
Clamour'd the livelong night: some say, the earth
Was feverous and did shake.
MACB. 'Twas a rough night.
LEN. My young rememberance cannot parallel.
A fellow to it.

[*Re-enter* MACDUFF.]

. . . **lie,** (1) floored you. (2) lied to you. **46. cast,** (1) throw, (2) throw up. **51. timely,** early. **52. slipp'd the hour,** missed the time. **55. physics,** cures. **57. limited service,** especially assigned duty. **58. appoint,** plan. **63. combustion,** social tumult. **64. obscure bird,** the bird which loves darkness, i.e., the owl. **66 feverous,** i.e., suffered from malaria.

MACD. O horror, horror, horror! Tongue nor heart
Cannot conceive nor name thee!

MACB. / LEN. What's the matter?

MACD. Confusion now hath made his masterpiece!
Most sacrilegious murder hath broke ope
The Lord's anointed temple, and stole thence
The life o' the building!

MACB. What is 't you say? the life?

LEN. Mean you his majesty?

MACD. Approach the chamber, and destroy your sight
With a new Gorgon: do not bid me speak;
See, and then speak yourselves.

[*Exeunt* MACBETH *and* LENNOX.]

Awake, awake!
Ring the alarum-bell. Murder and treason!
Banquo and Donalbain! Malcolm! awake!
Shake off this downy sleep, death's counterfeit,
And look on death itself! up, up, and see
The great doom's image! Malcolm! Banquo!
As from your graves rise up, and walk like sprites,
To countenance this horror! Ring the bell.

[*Bell rings.*

[*Enter* LADY MACBETH.]

LADY M. What's the business,
That such a hideous trumpet calls to parley
The sleepers of the house? speak, speak!

MACD. O gentle lady,
'Tis not for you to hear what I can speak:
The repetition, in a woman's ear,
Would murder as it fell.

71. **Confusion,** destruction. 73. **Lord's . . . temple,** i.e., the King's body. 77. **Gorgon,** Medusa, one of the three monsters in Greek mythology, the sight of whom turned the beholder into stone. 83. **great . . . image,** i.e., a thing resembling the horrors of Doomsday. 85. **countenance this horror,** give the horrible sight its proper setting.

[*Enter* BANQUO.]

O Banquo, Banquo,
Our royal master's murder'd!
LADY M. Woe, alas!
What, in our house?
BAN. Too cruel any where.
Dear Duff, I prithee, contradict thyself,
And say it is not so.

[*Re-enter* MACBETH *and* LENNOX, *with* ROSS.]

MACB. Had I but died an hour before this chance,
I had lived a blessèd time; for, from this instant,
There's nothing serious in mortality:
All is but toys: renown and grace is dead;
The wine of life is drawn, and the mere lees
Is left this vault to brag of.

[*Enter* MALCOLM *and* DONALBAIN.]

DON. What is amiss?
MACB. You are, and do not know 't:
The spring, the head, the fountain of your blood
Is stopp'd; the very source of it is stopp'd.
MACD. Your royal father's murdered.
MAL. O, by whom?
LEN. Those of his chamber, as it seem'd, had done 't:
Their hands and faces were all badged with blood;
So were their daggers, which unwiped we found
Upon their pillows:
They stared, and were distracted; no man's life
Was to be trusted with them.
MACB. O, yet I do repent me of my fury,
That I did kill them.
MACD. Wherefore did you so?
MACB. Who can be wise, amazed, temperate and furious,

90. repetition, telling. **98. serious in mortality,** important in human life. **103. head,** fountain head. **107. badged,** marked as with a badge.

Loyal and neutral, in a moment? No man:
The expedition of my violent love
Outrun the pauser, reason. Here lay Duncan,
His silver skin laced with his golden blood;
And his gash'd stabs look'd like a breach in nature
For ruin's wasteful entrance: there, the murderers,
Steep'd in the colours of their trade, their daggers
Unmannerly breech'd with gore: who could refrain,
That had a heart to love, and in that heart
Courage to make 's love known?

LADY M. Help me hence, ho!

MACD. Look to the lady.

MAL. [*Aside to* DON.] Why do we hold our tongues,
That most may claim this argument for ours?

DON. [*Aside to* MAL.] What should be spoken here, where our fate,
Hid in an auger-hole, may rush, and seize us?
Let's away;
Our tears are not yet brew'd.

MAL. [*Aside to* DON.] Nor our strong sorrow
Upon the foot of motion.

BAN. Look to the lady:

[LADY MACBETH *is carried out.*]

And when we have our naked frailties hid,
That suffer in exposure, let us meet,
And question this most bloody piece of work,
To know it further. Fears and scruples shake us:
In the great hand of God I stand; and thence
Against the undivulged pretence I fight
Of treasonous malice.

MACD. And so do I.

116. expedition, speed. **117. pauser reason,** reason which causes one to pause and deliberate. **119. breach,** a gap made in a city wall by an attacking army. **120. wasteful,** destructive. **122. unmannerly breech'd,** rudely covered to the hilt. **124. make's,** make his. **126. argument,** affair. **128. auger-hole,** i.e., an obscure hiding place. **131. Upon . . . motion,** ready to translate itself into action. **132-3. when . . . exposure,** when we have put on our clothes. **135. scruples,** hesitations.

ALL. So all.
MACB. Let's briefly put on manly readiness,
And meet i' the hall together.
ALL. Well contented.
[*Exeunt all but* MALCOLM *and* DONALBAIN.
MAL. What will you do? Let's not consort with them:
To show an unfelt sorrow is an office.
Which the false man does easy. I'll to England.
DON. To Ireland, I; our separated fortune
Shall keep us both the safer: where we are,
There's daggers in men's smiles: the near in blood,
The nearer bloody.
MAL. This murderous shaft that's shot
Hath not yet lighted, and our safest way
Is to avoid the aim. Therefore, to horse;
And let us not be dainty of leave-taking,
But shift away: there's warrant in that theft
Which steals itself, when there's no mercy left. [*Exeunt.*

SCENE IV. *Outside* MACBETH'S *castle.*

[*Enter* ROSS *and an* OLD MAN.]

OLD M. Threescore and ten I can remember well:
Within the volume of which time I have seen
Hours dreadful and things strange; but this sore night
Hath trifled former knowings.
ROSS. Ah, good father,
Thou seest, the heavens, as troubled with man's act,
Threaten his bloody stage: by the clock, 'tis day,
And yet dark night strangles the travelling lamp:
Is 't night's predominance, or the day's shame,

137. undivulged pretence, undiscovered purpose. **139. briefly,** quickly; **manly readiness,** male equipment, i.e., armor. **142. office,** action. **143. The false man,** any false man. **146-7. the near . . . bloody,** the nearer one's blood relationship to the King, the greater one's danger. **150. dainty of,** too particular about. **151. shift,** steal; **warrant,** justification. Scene iv: **4. trifled knowings,** dwarfed previous experiences. **6. bloody stage,** i.e., the earth. **7. travelling lamp,** the sun. **8-9. It's . . . shame,**

That darkness does the face of earth entomb,
When living light should kiss it?

OLD M. 'Tis unnatural,
Even like the deed that's done. On Tuesday last,
A falcon, towering in her pride of place,
Was by a mousing owl hawk'd at and kill'd.

ROSS. And Duncan's horses—a thing most strange and certain—
Beauteous and swift, the minions of their race,
Turn'd wild in nature, broke their stalls, flung out,
Contending 'gainst obedience, as they would make
War with mankind.

OLD M. 'Tis said they eat each other.

ROSS. They did so, to the amazement of mine eyes
That look'd upon 't. Here comes the good Macduff.

[*Enter* MACDUFF.]

How goes the world, sir, now?

MACD. Why, see you not?

ROSS. Is 't known who did this more than bloody deed?

MACD. Those that Macbeth hath slain.

ROSS. Alas, the day!
What good could they pretend?

MACD. They were suborn'd:
Malcolm and Donalbain, the king's two sons,
Are stol'n away and fled; which puts upon them
Suspicion of the deed.

ROSS. 'Gainst nature still!
Thriftless ambition, that wilt ravin up
Thine own life's means! Then 'tis most like
The sovereignty will fall upon Macbeth.

it is that darkness has become more powerful than the light of day, or that day is so ashamed of the deed that it will not show its face. **12. towering . . . place,** proudly soaring at the top of its flight. **15. minions,** darlings. **19. amazement,** stupefaction. **24. pretend,** allege; **suborn'd, bribed** (to commit the crime). **28. ravin up,** devour raven-

MACD. He is already named, and gone to Scone
To be invested.
ROSS. Where is Duncan's body.
MACD. Carried to Colmekill,
The sacred storehouse of his predecessors,
And guardian of their bones.
ROSS. Will you to Scone?
MACD. No, cousin, I'll to Fife.
ROSS. Well, I will thither.
MACD. Well, may you see things well done there: adieu!
Lest our old robes sit easier than our new!
ROSS. Farewell, father.
OLD MAN. God's benison go with you; and with those
That would make good of bad, and friends of foes! [*Exeunt.*

ACT III

SCENE I. *Forres. The palace.*

[*Enter* BANQUO.]

BAN. Thou hast it now: king, Cawdor, Glamis, all,
As the weird women promised, and, I fear,
Thou play'dst most foully for 't: yet it was said
It should not stand in thy posterity,
But that myself should be the root and father
Of many kings. If there come truth from them—
As upon thee, Macbeth, their speeches shine—
Why, by the verities on thee made good,
May they not be my oracles as well,
And set up in hope? But hush! no more.

ously. **31. Scone,** ancient capital of Scotland. **33. Colmekill,** the island Iona, where Scottish kings were once buried. **36. Fife,** Macduff's castle; **thither,** i.e., to Scone. **40. benison,** blessing. **Act III, Scene i: 4. stand . . . posterity,** continue with your descendants. **7. shine,** are brilliantly clear. **9. oracles,** prophets. **s.d. Sennet,** trumpet call.

[*Sennet sounded. Enter* MACBETH, *as king*, LADY MACBETH, *as queen*, LENNOX, ROSS, LORDS, LADIES, *and* ATTENDANTS.]

MACB. Here's our chief guest.
LADY M. If he had been forgotten,
It had been as a gap in our great feast,
And all-thing unbecoming.
MACB. To-night we hold a solemn supper, sir,
And I'll request your presence.
BAN. Let your highness
Command upon me; to the which my duties
Are with a most indissoluble tie
For ever knit.
MACB. Ride you this afternoon?
BAN. Ay, my good lord.
MACB. We should have else desired your good advice,
Which still hath been both grave and prosperous,
In this day's council; but we'll take to-morrow.
Is 't far you ride?
BAN. As far, my lord, as will fill up the time
'Twixt this and supper: go not my horse the better,
I must become a borrower of the night
For a dark hour or twain.
MACB. Fail not our feast.
BAN. My lord, I will not.
MACB. We hear, our bloody cousins are bestow'd
In England and in Ireland, not confessing
Their cruel parricide, filling their hearers
With strange invention: but of that to-morrow,
When therewithal we shall have cause of state
Craving us jointly. Hie you to horse: adieu,
Till you return at night. Goes Fleance with you?

13. **all things,** altogether. 14. **solemn supper,** formal banquet. 16. **which,** i.e., your command. 22. **prosperous,** productive of good results. 26. **go . . . better,** unless my horse goes faster (than I expect). 30. **are bestow'd,** have taken refuge. 33. **invention,** i.e., lies. 34. **therewithal,** besides that; **cause of state,** official business. 35. **Craving us**

BAN. Ay, my good lord: our time does call upon 's.
MACB. I wish your horses swift and sure of foot;
And so I do commend you to their backs.
Farewell. [*Exit* BANQUO.]
Let every man be master of his time
Till seven at night: to make society
The sweeter welcome, we will keep ourself
Till supper-time alone: while then, God be with you!
[*Exeunt all but* MACBETH *and an* ATTENDANT.]
Sirrah, a word with you: attend those men
Our pleasure?
ATTEN. They are, my lord, without the palace gate.
MACB. Bring them before us.
[*Exit* ATTENDANT.]
To be thus is nothing;
But to be safely thus.—Our fears in Banquo
Stick deep; and in his royalty of nature
Reigns that which would be fear'd: 'tis much he dares;
And, to that dauntless temper of his mind,
He hath a wisdom that doth guide his valour
To act in safety. There is none but he
Whose being I do fear: and, under him,
My Genius is rebuked; as, it is said,
Mark Antony's was by Cæsar. He chid the sisters
When first they put the name of king upon me,
And bade them speak to him: then prophet-like
They hail'd him father to a line of kings:
Upon my head they placed a fruitless crown,
And put a barren sceptre in my gripe,
Thence to be wrench'd with an unlineal hand,
No son of mine succeeding, If 't be so,

jointly, demanding the attention of both of us; **Hie,** hasten. **37. our . . . upon's,** we are pressed for time. **43. keep ourself,** stay by myself. **44. while,** until; **attend . . . pleasure,** are those men waiting for me? **48. thus,** i.e., King. **49. But to be,** unless we are. **50. Stick deep,** have their roots deep in his nature. **51. would,** must. **52. to,** added to **55. being,** existence. **56. Genius,** guiding spirit. **62. gripe,** grasp.

For Banquo's issue have I filed my mind;
For them the gracious Duncan have I murder'd;
Put rancours in the vessel of my peace
Only for them; and mine eternal jewel
Given to the common enemy of man,
To make them kings, the seed of Banquo kings!
Rather than so, come fate into the list,
And champion me to the utterance! Who's there?

[*Re-enter* ATTENDANT, *with two* MURDERERS.]

Now go to the door, and stay there till we call.
[*Exit* ATTENDANT.]
Was it not yesterday we spoke together?
FIRST MUR. It was, so please your highness.
MACB. Well then, now
Have you consider'd of my speeches? Know
That it was he in the times past which held you
So under fortune, which you thought had been
Our innocent self: this I made good to you
In our last conference, pass'd in probation with you,
How you were borne in hand, how cross'd the instruments,
Who wrought with them, and all things else that might
To half a soul and to a notion crazed
Say "Thus did Banquo."
FIRST MUR. You made it known to us.
MACB. I did so, and went further, which is now
Our point of second meeting. Do you find
Your patience so predominant in your nature
That you can let this go? Are you so gospell'd
To pray for this good man and for his issue,

63. unlineal hand, hand of one not descended from me. **65. filed,** defiled. **68. eternal jewel,** i.e., immortal soul. **69. Common . . . man,** the devil. **72. champion . . . utterance,** challenge me to mortal combat. **77-8. held . . . fortune,** kept you so unfortunate. **79. made good,** proved. **80. pass'd . . . probation,** gone over and approved. **81. borne in hand,** deceived; **instruments,** means by which it was accomplished. **83. half a soul,** a half-wit; **notion,** mind. **86. Our meeting,** the point of our second meeting. **88. gospell'd,** under the influence of the Gospel com-

Whose heavy hand hath bow'd you to the grave
And beggar'd yours for ever?
FIRST MUR. We are men, my liege.
MACB. Ay, in the catalogue ye go for men;
As hounds and greyhounds, mongrels, spaniels, curs,
Shoughs, water-rugs and demi-wolves are clept
All by the name of dogs: the valued file
Distinguishes the swift, the slow, the subtle,
The housekeeper, the hunter, every one
According to the gift which bounteous nature
Hath in him closed, whereby he does receive
Particular addition, from the bill
That writes them all alike: and so of men.
Now, if you have a station in the file,
Not i' the worst rank of manhood, say 't;
And I will put that business in your bosoms,
Whose executions takes your enemy off,
Grapples you to the heart and love of us,
Who wear our health but sickly in his life,
Which in his death were perfect.
SEC. MUR. I am one, my liege,
Whom the vile blows and buffets of the world
Have so incensed that I am reckless what
I do to spite the world.
FIRST MUR. And I another
So weary with disaster, tugg'd with fortune,
That I would set my life on any chance,
To mend it, or be rid on 't.
MACB. Both of you
Know Banquo was your enemy.

mand to "pray for them which despitefully use you," Matt. V. 44. **91. yours,** your families. **92. catalogue,** list; **go,** pass. **94. Shoughs,** pronounced ("shocks") shaggy Icelandic dogs; **water-rugs,** shaggy water dogs; **clept,** called. **95. valued file,** list enumerating the points of each breed. **96 subtle,** clever. **97. housekeeper,** watch dog. **100. addition,** mark of distinction; **from,** differing from; **bill,** list. **101. writes . . . alike,** puts them down indiscriminately.

BOTH. MUR. True, my lord.
MACB. So is he mine; and in such bloody distance,
That every minute of his being thrusts
Against my near'st of life: and though I could
With barefaced power sweep him from my sight
And bid my will avouch it, yet I must not,
For certain friends that are both his and mine,
Whose loves I may not drop, but wail his fall
Who I myself struck down; and thence it is,
That I to your assistance do make love,
Masking the business from the common eye
For sundry weighty reasons.
SEC. MUR. We shall, my lord,
Perform what you command us.
FIRST MUR. Though our lives—
MACB. Your spirits shine through you. Within this hour at most
I will advise you where to plant yourselves;
Acquaint you with the perfect spy o' the time,
The moment on 't; for 't must be done tonight,
And something from the palace; always thought
That I require a clearness: and with him—
To leave no ribs nor botches in the work—
Fleance his son, that keeps him company,
Whose absence is no less material to me
Than is his father's, must embrace the fate
Of that dark hour. Resolve yourselves apart:
I'll come to you anon.
BOTH MUR. We are resolved, my lord.
MACB. I'll call upon you straight: abide within.

112. tugg'd with, mauled by. **113. set,** stake. **116. distance,** enmity. **118. near'st of life,** most vital parts. **119. barefaced,** i.e., open exercise of. **120. avouch,** justify. **121. For,** because of. **122. but wail,** instead of that I must bewail. **125. common,** public. **130. the . . . time,** exact information as to the best time (for the murder). **131. on't,** for it. **132. something,** some distance; **always thought,** let it be clearly understood. **133. clearness,** freedom from being suspected. **134. rubs,** hindrances. **136. material,** important. **138. Resolve . . . apart,** make up your minds

[*Exeunt* MURDERERS.]

It is concluded. Banquo, they soul's flight,
If it find heaven, must find it out to-night. [*Exit.*

SCENE II. *The palace.*

[*Enter* LADY MACBETH *and a* SERVANT.]

LADY M. Is Banquo gone from court?
SERV. Ay, madam, but returns again tonight.
LADY M. Say to the king, I would attend his leisure
For a few words.
SERV. Madam, I will. [*Exit.*
LADY M. Nought's had, all's spent,
Where our desire is got without content:
'Tis safer to be that which we destroy
Than by destruction dwell in doubtful joy.

[*Enter* MACBETH.]

How now, my lord! why do you keep alone,
Of sorriest fancies your companions making,
Using those thoughts which should indeed have died
With them they think on? Things without all remedy
Should be without regard: what's done is done.
MACB. We have scotch'd the snake, not kill'd it:
She'll close and be herself, whilst our poor malice
Remains in danger of her former tooth.
But let the frame of things disjoint, both the worlds suffer,
Ere we will eat our meal in fear and sleep
In the affliction of these terrible dreams
That shake us nightly: better be with the dead,
Whom we, to gain our peace, have sent to peace,

by yourselves. **Scene ii: 11. without,** beyond. **12. without regard,** i.e., should not be thought about. **13. scotch'd,** cut in two. **14. close . . . herself,** reunite and be whole again; poor, feeble. **15. former tooth,** her fang which could have poisoned us (before we cut her in two). **16. the frame . . . disjoint,** the universe go to pieces; **both . . . suffer,** i.e., both this world and the next be destroyed. **22. restless ecstasy,** a frenzy of unrest.

Than on the torture of the mind to lie
In restless ecstasy. Duncan is in his grave;
After life's fitful fever he sleeps well;
Treason has done his worst: nor steel, nor poison,
Malice domestic, foreign levy, nothing,
Can touch him further.

LADY M. Come on;
Gentle my lord, sleek o'er your rugged looks;
Be bright and jovial among your guests tonight.

MACB. So shall I, love; and so, I pray, be you:
Let your remembrance apply to Banquo;
Present him eminence, both with eye and tongue:
Unsafe the while, that we
Must lave our honours in these flattering streams,
And make our faces vizards to our hearts,
Disguising what they are.

LADY M. You must leave this.

MACB. O, full of scorpions is my mind, dear wife!
Thou know'st that Banquo, and his Fleance, lives.

LADY M. But in them nature's copy's not eterne.

MACB. There's comfort yet; they are assailable;
Then be thou jocund: ere the bat hath flown
His cloister'd flight, ere to black Hecate's summons
The shard-borne beetle with his drowsy hums
Hath rung night's yawning peal, there shall be done
A deed of dreadful note.

LADY M. What's to be done?

MACB. Be innocent of the knowledge, dearest chuck,
Till thou applaud the deed. Come, seeling night,
Scarf up the tender eye of pitiful day;

25. Malice domestic, civil discord; **foreign levy,** attack from abroad. **27. sleek . . . looks,** smooth your wrinkled brow. **31. Present him eminence,** distinguish him with special attentions. **32. Unsafe . . . we,** unsafe as long as we. **33. lave . . . streams,** wash our honors in streams of flattery. **34. vizards,** masks. **38. nature's . . . eterne,** man holds only a temporary lease (copy) on life, not a perpetual one. **41. cloister'd, in cloisters,** i.e., in darkness and loneliness. **42. shard-borne,** borne on scaly wings. **43. yawning peal,** summons to sleep. **45. chuck,**

And with thy bloody and invisible hand
Cancel and tear to pieces that great bond
Which keeps me pale! Light thickens; and the crow
Makes wings to the rooky wood:
Good things of day begin to droop and drowse;
Whiles night's black agents to their preys do rouse.
Thou marvell'st at my words: but hold thee still:
Things bad begun make strong themselves by ill.
So, prithee, go with me. [*Exeunt.*

SCENE III. *A park near the palace.*

[*Enter three* MURDERERS.]

FIRST MUR. But who did bid thee join with us?
THIRD MUR. Macbeth.
SEC. MUR. He needs not our mistrust, since he delivers
Our offices and what we have to do
To the direction just.
FIRST MUR. Then stand with us.
The west yet glimmers with some streaks of day:
Now spurs the lated traveller apace
To gain the timely inn; and near approaches
The subject of our watch.
THIRD MUR. Hark! I hear horses.
BAN. [*within*] Give us a light there, ho!
SEC. MUR. Then 'tis he: the rest
That are within the note of expectation
Already are i' the court.
FIRST MUR. His horses go about.

chick. **46. seeling,** to seel was to sew up the eyelids of a young falcon during its training, hence blinding. **47. Scarf up,** blindfold. **49. great bond,** the bond which binds Banquo to life. **51. rooky,** inhabited by rooks, English crows; hence gloomy. **54. hold thee still,** say nothing. **Scene iii: 2. He . . . mistrust,** we need not distrust him (the third murderer). **2-4. he delivers . . . just,** reports our particular functions and duties exactly as we have been instructed (by Macbeth). **6. lated,** belated. **7. timely inn,** inn in good season. **8. subject . . . watch,** person for whom we wait. **10. within . . . expectation,** on the list of expected guests. **11. go about,** go around (by the road).

THIRD MUR. Almost a mile: but he does usually,
So all men do, from hence to the palace gate
Make it their walk.

SEC. MUR. A light, a light!

[*Enter* BANQUO, *and* FLEANCE *with a torch.*]

THIRD MUR. 'Tis he.

FIRST MUR. Stand to 't.

BAN. It will be rain to-night.

FIRST MUR. Let it come down.

[*They set upon* BANQUO.

BAN. O, treachery! Fly, good Fleance, fly, fly, fly!
Thou mayst revenge. O slave!

[*Dies.* FLEANCE *escapes.*

THIRD MUR. Who did strike out the light?

FIRST MUR. Was't not the way?

THIRD MUR. There's but one down; the son is fled.

SEC. MUR. We have lost
Best half of our affair.

FIRST MUR. Well, let's away, and say how much is done.

[*Exeunt.*

SCENE IV. *The same. Hall in the palace.*

[*A banquet prepared. Enter* MACBETH, LADY MACBETH, ROSS, LENNOX, LORDS, *and* ATTENDANTS.]

MACB. You know your own degrees; sit down: at first
And last the hearty welcome.

LORDS. Thanks to your majesty.

MACB. Ourself will mingle with society,
And play the humble host.
Our hostess keeps her state, but in best time

Scene iv: 1. degrees, ranks. **1-2. at first And last,** once and for all (i.e., until the end of the feast). **3. mingle with society,** i.e., descend from the dais and talk with everyone. **5. keeps her state,** remains seated apart on her chair of state; **in best time,** at the proper moment. **6. require her welcome,** ask her to make a speech of welcome.

We will require her welcome.
LADY M. Pronounce it for me, sir, to all our friends;
For my heart speaks they are welcome.

[*First* MURDERER *appears at the door.*]

MACB. See, they encounter thee with their hearts' thanks.
Both sides are even: here I'll sit i' the midst:
Be large in mirth; anon we'll drink a measure
The table round. [*Approaching the door.*] There's blood upon thy face.
MUR. 'Tis Banquo's then.
MACB. 'Tis better thee without than he within.
Is he dispatch'd?
MUR. My lord, his throat is cut; that I did for him.
MACB. Thou art the best o' the cut-throats: yet he's good
That did the like for Fleance: if thou didst it.
Thou art the nonpareil.
MUR. Most royal sir,
Fleance is 'scaped.
MACB. Then comes my fit again: I had else been perfect,
Whole as the marble, founded as the rock,
As broad and general as the casing air:
But now I am cabin'd, cribb'd, confined, bound in
To saucy doubts and fears. But Banquo's safe?
MUR. Ay, my good lord: safe in a ditch he bides,
With twenty trenchèd gashes on his head;
The least a death to nature.
MACB. Thanks for that.
There the grown serpent lies; the worm that's fled
Hath nature that in time will venom breed,

9. **encounter,** respond to. 10. **Both . . . even,** the seats on both sides of the table are filled. 11. **large,** unrestrained. 11-2. **measure . . . round,** a health to each one around the table. 14. **thee . . . within,** to have his blood outside you than in him. 21. **fit,** seizure of fear; **perfect,** perfectly satisfied. 22. **founded,** firmly based. 23. **general,** unconfined; **casing,** surrounding. 24. **cribb'd,** boxed up. 24-5 **bound in To,** imprisoned along with. 25. **saucy,** annoying. 29. **worm,** little snake. 32. **hear our-**

No teeth for the present. Get thee gone: tomorrow
We'll hear ourselves again. [*Exit* MURDERER.

LADY M. My royal lord,
You do not give the cheer: the feast is sold
That is not often vouch'd, while 'tis a-making,
'Tis given with welcome: to feed were best at home;
From thence the sauce to meat is ceremony;
Meeting were bare without it.

MACB. Sweet remembrancer!
Now, good digestion wait on appetite,
And health on both!

LEN. May 't please your highness sit.

[*The Ghost of* BANQUO *enters, and sits in* MACBETH'S *place.*

MACB. Here had we now our country's honour roof'd,
Were the graced person of our Banquo present;
Who may I rather challenge for unkindness
Than pity for mischance!

ROSS. His absence, sir,
Lays blame upon his promise. Please 't your highness
To grace us with your royal company.

MACB. The table's full.

LEN. Here is a place reserved, sir.

MACB. Where?

LEN. Here, my good lord. What is 't that moves your highness?

MACB. Which of you have done this?

LORDS. What, my good lord?

MACB. Thou canst not say I did it: never shake
Thy gory locks at me.

selves, confer with each other. **33. give the cheer,** play the part of host (by drinking healths). **33-5. the feast . . . welcome,** i.e., unless a host at a banquet frequently affirms his welcome by fitting ceremony he might as well be an innkeeper and sell his food. **35. to feed . . . home,** i.e., if one eats merely to fill one's stomach, one had better stay at home. **36. From . . . ceremony,** away from home formal politeness is the best sauce for food. **37. remembrancer,** one who reminds me (of my duty). **40. country's . . . roof'd,** all the nobility of our country under one roof.

ROSS. Gentlemen rise; his highness is not well.
LADY M. Sit, worthy friends: my lord is often thus,
And hath been from his youth: pray you, keep seat;
The fit is momentary; upon a thought
He will again be well: if much you note him,
You shall offend him and extend his passion:
Feed, and regard him not. Are you a man?
MACB. Ay, and a bold one, that dare look on that
Which might appal the devil.
LADY M. O proper stuff!
This is the very painting of your fear:
This is the air-drawn dagger which, you said,
Led you to Duncan. O, these flaws and starts,
Imposters to true fear, would well become
A woman's story at a winter's fire,
Authorized by her grandam. Shame itself!
Why do you make such faces? When all's done,
You look but on a stool.
MACB. Prithee, see there! behold! look! lo! how say you?
Why, what care I? If thou canst nod, speak too.
If charnel-houses and our graves must send
Those that we bury back, our monuments
Shall be the maws of kites. [GHOST *vanishes.*
LADY M. What, quite unmann'd in folly?
MACB. If I stand here, I saw him.
LADY M. Fie, for shame!
MACB. Blood hath been shed ere now, i' the olden time,
Ere humane statue purged the gentle weal;

55. upon a thought, in an instant. **57. extend,** prolong. **60. proper stuff,** mere rubbish. **61. very painting,** nothing but the creation. **63. flaws,** gusts (of passion). **64. to,** when compared to. **66. Authorized . . . grandam,** citing her grandmother as her authority. **68. You . . . stool,** you see only an empty chair. **69. how say you,** what do you say to that? **71. charnel-houses,** small buildings in which were preserved skulls and other bones exhumed in digging new graves. **72. monuments,** graves. **73. maws of kites,** stomachs of hawks. **76. humane . . . weal,** benevolent laws civilized the state by purging it (of violence).

Ay, and since too, murders have been perform'd
Too terrible for the ear: the time has been,
That, when the brains were out, the man would die,
And there an end; but now they rise again,
With twenty mortal murders on their crowns,
And push us from our stools: this is more strange
Than such a murder is.

LADY M. My worthy lord,
Your noble friends do lack you.

MACB. I do forget.
Do not muse at me, my most worthy friends:
I have a strange infirmity, which is nothing
To those that know me. Come, love and health to all;
Then I'll sit down. Give me some wine; fill full.
I drink to the general joy o' the whole table,
And to our dear friend Banquo, whom we miss;
Would he were here! to all, and him, we thirst,
And all to all.

LORDS. Our duties, and the pledge.

[*Re-enter* GHOST.]

MACB. Avaunt! and quit my sight! let the earth hide thee!
Thy bones are marrowless, thy blood is cold;
Thou hast no speculation in those eyes
Which thou dost glare with!

LADY M. Think of this, good peers,
But as a thing of custom: 'tis no other;
Only it spoils the pleasure of the time.

MACB. What man dare, I dare:
Approach thou like the rugged Russian bear,
The arm'd rhinoceros, or the Hyrcan tiger;
Take any shape but that, and my firm nerves

81. twenty . . . murders, twenty gashes each one of which could cause death. **84. lack you,** miss your company. **85. muse,** wonder. **91. thirst,** thirst to drink to. **92. all to all,** i.e., let us all drink to the whole company. **92. Our . . . pledge,** our homage to you and a health (to Banquo). **93. Avaunt,** get thee gone. **95. speculation,** intelligent expression. **100. rugged,** fierce. **101. Hyrcan,** of Hyrcania, a country south of the

Shall never tremble: or be alive again,
And dare me to the desert with thy sword;
If trembling I inhabit then, protest me
The baby of a girl. Hence, horrible shadow!
Unreal mockery, hence! [GHOST *vanishes.*]
Why, so: being gone
I am a man again. Pray you, sit still.

LADY M. You have displaced the mirth, broke the good meeting,
With most admired disorder.

MACB. Can such things be,
And overcome us like a summer's cloud,
Without our special wonder? You make me strange
Even to the disposition that I owe.
When now I think you can behold such sights,
And keep the natural ruby of your cheeks,
When mine is blanch'd with fear.

ROSS. What sights, my lord?

LADY M. I pray you, speak not; he grows worse and worse;
Question enrages him. At once, good night:
Stand not upon the order of your going,
But go at once.

LEN. Good night; and better health
Attend his majesty!

LADY M. A kind good night to all!
[*Exeunt all but* MACBETH *and* LADY M.

MACB. It will have blood; they say, blood will have blood:
Stones have been known to move and trees to speak;
Augurs and understood relations have
By magot-pies and choughs and rooks brought forth

Caspian Sea where tigers were supposed to abound. **105. If . . . then,** if then I put on trembling (as a garment). **105-6. protest . . . girl,** proclaim me an infant of an immature mother, hence, a weakling. **110. admired disorder,** amazing lack of self-control. **111. overcome . . . cloud,** surprise us no more than the passing of a summer's cloud. **112. strange,** unfamiliar. **113. owe,** own. **119. Stand . . . going,** do not insist on leaving in order of your rank. **124. understood relations,** reports the significance of which is properly understood. **125. By magot-**

The secret'st man of blood. What is the night?
LADY M. Almost at odds with morning, which is which.
MACB. How say'st thou, that Macduff denies his person
At our great bidding?
LADY M. Did you send to him, sir?
MACB. I hear it by the way; but I will send:
There's not a one of them but in his house
I keep a servant fee'd. I will to-morrow,
And betimes I will, to the weird sisters:
More shall they speak; for now I am bent to know,
By the worst means, the worst. For mine own good,
All causes shall give way: I am in blood
Stepp'd in so far that, should I wade no more,
Returning were as tedious as go o'er:
Strange things I have in head, that will to hand;
Which must be acted ere they may be scann'd.
LADY M. You lack the season of all natures, sleep.
MACB. Come, we'll to sleep. My strange and self-abuse
Is the initiate fear that wants hard use:
We are yet but young in deed. [*Exeunt.*

SCENE V. *A Heath.*

[*Thunder. Enter the three* WITCHES, *meeting* HECATE.]

FIRST WITCH. Why, how now, Hecate! you look angerly.
HEC. Have I not reason, beldams as you are,
Saucy and overbold? How did you dare
To trade and traffic with Macbeth

pies, by means of magpies (relatives of blue jays); **forth,** to light. **126. secret'st . . . blood,** the least suspected murderer. **What . . . night?** What time of night is it? **127. at odds with,** in dispute with, i.e., it is daybreak. **128 denies his person,** refuses to appear. **130. by the way,** indirectly. **131. them,** i.e., the nobles. **132. servant fee'd,** a paid spy. **133. betimes,** early. **134. bent,** eager, like a taut bow-string. **136. causes,** considerations. **140. scann'd,** considered, weighed. **141. season,** preservative. **142-3. My strange . . . use,** i.e., my strange self-deception (in thinking I saw ghosts) springs from the fear to which a novice (in crime) is prey, and it can be stilled only by much practice (in crime). **Scene v:** This scene is almost surely not by Shakespeare. **s.d. Hecate,** goddess of witchcraft. **2. beldams,** hags.

In riddles and affairs of death;
And I, the mistress of your charms,
The close contriver of all harms,
Was never call'd to bear my part,
Or show the glory of our art?
And, which is worse, all you have done
Hath been but for a wayward son,
Spiteful and wrathful, who, as others do,
Loves for his own ends, not for you.
But make amends now: get you gone,
And at the pit of Acheron
Meet me i' the morning: thither he
Will come to know his destiny:
Your vessels and your spells provide,
Your charms and every thing beside.
I am for the air; this night I'll spend
Unto a dismal and a fatal end:
Great business must be wrought ere noon;
Upon the corner of the moon
There hangs a vaporous drop profound;
I'll catch it ere it come to ground:
And that distill'd by magic sleights
Shall raise such artificial sprites
As by the strength of their illusion
Shall draw him on to his confusion:
He shall spurn fate, scorn death, and bear
His hopes 'bove wisdom, grace and fear:
And you all know, security
Is mortals' chiefest enemy.
[*Music and a song within*: "Come away, come away," &c.]
Hark! I am call'd; my little spirit, see,
Sits in a foggy cloud, and stays for me.

7. **close,** secret. 15. **Acheron,** river in Hades. 24. **profound,** of hidden powers. 27. **artificial,** produced by magical artifice. 29. **confusion,** ruin. 32. **security,** overconfidence. **Scene vi:** 3. **borne,** managed. 8. **want the thought,** help thinking. 21. **from,** because of; **broad,** plain. 25. **holds,** withholds. 27. **Edward,** Edward the Confessor. 30. **upon his aid,** i.e.,

[*Exit.*

FIRST WITCH. Come, let's make haste; she'll soon be back again. [*Exeunt.*

SCENE VI. *Forres. The palace.*

[*Enter* LENNOX *and another* LORD.]

LEN. My former speeches have but hit your thoughts,
Which can interpret further: only, I say,
Things have been strangely borne. The gracious Duncan
Was pitied on Macbeth: marry, he was dead:
And the right-valiant Banquo walk'd too late;
Whom, you may say, if't please you, Fleance kill'd,
For Fleance fled: men must not walk too late.
Who cannot want the thought how monstrous
It was for Malcolm and for Donalbain
To kill their gracious father? damnèd fact!
How it did grieve Macbeth! did he not straight
In pious rage the two delinquents tear,
That were the slaves of drink and thralls of sleep?
Was not that nobly done? Ay, and wisely too;
For 'twould have anger'd any heart alive
To hear the men deny 't. So that, I say,
He has borne all things well: and I do think
That had he Duncan's sons under his key—
As, an 't please heaven, he shall not—they should find
What 'twere to kill a father; so should Fleance.
But, peace! for from broad words and' cause he fail'd
His presence at the tyrant's feast, I hear
Macduff lives in disgrace: sir, can you tell
Where he bestows himself?

LORD. The son of Duncan,
From whom this tyrant holds the due of birth,
Lives in the English court, and is received

for aid to Malcolm. **36. free,** freely bestowed. **40. absolute,** positive, curt.

Of the most pious Edward with such grace
That the malevolence of fortune nothing
Takes from his high respect: thither Macduff
Is gone to pray the holy king, upon his aid
To wake Northumberland and warlike Siward:
That, by the help of these—with Him above
To ratify the work—we may again
Give to our tables meat, sleep to our nights,
Free from our feasts and banquets bloody knives,
Do faithful homage and receive free honours:
All which we pine for now: and this report
Hath so exasperate the king that he
Prepares for some attempt of war.

LEN. Sent he to Macduff?

LORD. He did: and with an absolute "Sir, not I,"
The cloudy messenger turns me his back,
And hums, as who should say "You'll rue the time
That clogs me with this answer."

LEN. And that well might
Advise him to a caution, to hold what distance
His wisdom can provide. Some holy angel
Fly to the court of England and unfold
His message ere he come, that a swift blessing
May soon return to this our suffering country
Under a hand accursed!

LORD. I'll send my prayers with him.

[*Exeunt.*

ACT IV

SCENE I. *A cavern. In the middle, a boiling cauldron.*

[*Thunder. Enter the three* WITCHES.]

FIRST WITCH. Thrice the brinded cat hath mew'd.

41. cloudy, sullen. **Act IV, Scene i: 1. brinded,** brindled. **2. hedge-pig,** hedgehog. **3. Harpier,** name of an attendant evil spirit, perhaps sug-

SEC. WITCH. Thrice and once the hedge-pig whined.
THIRD WITCH. Harpier cries 'Tis time, 'tis time.
FIRST WITCH. Round about the cauldron go;
In the poison'd entrails throw.
Toad, that under cold stone
Days and nights has thirty one
Swelter'd venom sleeping got,
Boil thou first i' the charmèd pot.
ALL. Double, double toil and trouble;
Fire burn, and cauldron bubble.
SEC WITCH. Fillet of a fenny snake,
In the cauldron boil and bake;
Eye of newt and toe of frog,
Wool of bat and tongue of dog,
Adder's fork and blind-worm's sting,
Lizard's leg and howlet's wing,
For a charm of powerful trouble,
Like a hell-broth boil and bubble.
ALL. Double, double toil and trouble;
Fire burn and cauldron bubble.
THIRD WITCH. Scale of dragon, tooth of wolf,
Witches' mummy, maw and gulf
Of the ravin'd salt-sea shark,
Root of hemlock digg'd i' the dark,
Liver of blaspheming Jew,
Gall of goat, and slips of yew
Sliver'd in the moon's eclipse,
Nose of Turk and Tartar's lips,
Finger of birth-strangled babe
Ditch-deliver'd by a drab,
Make the gruel thick and slab:

gested by "harpy." **8. Swelter'd . . . got,** accumulated poison exuded in sweat. **12. Fillet . . . snake,** slice of a snake living in a fen or marsh. **16. fork,** forked tongue; **blind-worm,** a small limbless lizard mistakenly thought to be blind. **17. howlet's,** owl's. **23. Witches' mummy,** medicine made from a **mummy, maw and gulf,** stomach and gullet. **24. ravin'd,** ravenous. **28. Sliver'd,** broken off, like a branch. **30. birth-strangled,** strangled at birth and so unbaptized and a child

Add thereto a tiger's chaudron,
For the ingredients of our cauldron.
ALL. Double, double toil and trouble;
Fire burn and cauldron bubble.
SEC WITCH. Cool it with a baboon's blood,
Then the charm is firm and good.

[*Enter* HECATE *to the other three* WITCHES.]

HEC. O, well done! I commend your pains;
And every one shall share i' the gains:
And now about the cauldron sing,
Like elves and fairies in a ring,
Enchanting all that you put in.
[*Music and a song:* "Black spirits," &c.
[HECATE *retires.*

SEC. WITCH. By the pricking of my thumbs,
Something wicked this way comes.
Open locks,
Whoever knocks!

[*Enter* MACBETH.]

MACB. How now, you secret, black, and midnight hags!
What is 't you do?
ALL. A deed without a name.
MACB. I conjure you, by that which you profess,
Howe'er you come to know it, answer me:
Though you untie the winds and let them fight
Against the churches; though the yesty waves
Confound and swallow navigation up;
Though bladed corn be lodged and trees blown down;
Though castles topple on their warders' heads;
Though palaces and pyramids do slope
Their heads to their foundations; though the treasure

of the Devil. **31. Ditch-deliver'd,** born in a ditch; drab, harlot. **32. slab,** sticky. **33. chaudron,** entrails. **50. conjure,** solemnly command; **that . . . profess,** i.e., your witch's power of prophecy. **53. yesty,** foaming. **55. bladed . . . lodged,** wheat not yet in ear be blown flat. **56. warders,**

Of nature's germens tumble all together,
Even till destruction sicken; answer me
To what I ask you.

FIRST WITCH. Speak.

SEC. WITCH. Demand.

THIRD WITCH. We'll answer.

FIRST WITCH. Say, if thou'dst rather hear it from our mouths,
Or from our masters?

MACB. Call 'em; let me see 'em.

FIRST WITCH. Pour in sow's blood, that hath eaten
Her nine farrow; grease that's sweaten
From the murderer's gibbet throw
Into the flame.

ALL. Come, high or low;
Thyself and office deftly show!

[*Thunder. First* APPARITION: *an armed Head.*]

MACB. Tell me, thou unknown power,—

FIRST WITCH. He knows thy thought:
Hear his speech, but say thou nought.

FIRST APP. Macbeth! Macbeth! Macbeth! beware Macduff;
Beware the thane of Fife. Dismiss me.
Enough. [*Descends.*

MACB. Whate'er thou art, for thy good caution, thanks;
Thou hast harp'd my fear aright: but one word more,—

FIRST WITCH. He will not be commanded: here's another,
More potent than the first.

[*Thunder. Second* APPARITION: *a bloody Child.*]

guards'. 57. **pyramids,** possibly church steeples, which are shaped like pyramids. 58. **treasure,** accumulated store. 59. **nature's germens,** seeds of all living matter. 60. **sicken,** i.e., from excess. 65. **farrow,** litter of pigs. 67. **high or low,** from earth or from hell. 68. **office,** duties of your office. **s.d. armed Head,** this symbolizes the head of Macbeth cut off by Macduff. 74. **harp'd . . . aright,** played in tune with my fear. **s.d. bloody**

SEC. APP. Macbeth! Macbeth! Macbeth!
MACB. Had I three ears, I'ld hear thee.
SEC. APP. Be bloody, bold, and resolute; laugh to scorn
The power of man, for none of woman born
Shall harm Macbeth. [*Descends.*
MACB. Then live, Macduff: what need I fear of thee?
But yet I'll make assurance double sure,
And take a bond of fate: thou shalt not live;
That I may tell pale-hearted fear it lies,
And sleep in spite of thunder.

[*Thunder: Third* APPARITION: *a Child crowned, with a tree in his hand.*]

What is this
That rises like the issue of a king,
And wears upon his baby-brow the round
And top of sovereignty?
ALL. Listen, but speak not to 't.
THIRD APP. Be lion-mettled, proud; and take no care
Who chafes, who frets, or where conspirers are:
Macbeth shall never vanquish'd be until
Great Birnam wood to high Dunsinane hill
Shall come against him. [*Descends.*
MACB. That will never be:
Who can impress the forest, bid the tree
Unfix his earth-bound root? Sweet bodements! good!
Rebellion's head, rise never till the wood
Of Birnam rise, and our high-placed Macbeth
Shall live the lease of nature, pay his breath
To time and mortal custom. Yet my heart
Throbs to know one thing: tell me, if your art
Can tell so much: shall Banquo's issue ever

Child, i.e., Macduff, torn from his mother's womb. **85. That,** so that. **s.d. Child, Malcolm,** whose soldiers were to cover themselves with boughs. **88-89. round . . . sovereignty,** i.e., the crown. **95. impress,** draft (for military service. **96. bodements,** prophecies. **99. live . . . nature,** a life of normal length). **99-100. pay . . . custom,** die at the customary age.

Reign in this kingdom?
ALL. Seek to know no more.
MACB. I will be satisfied: deny me this,
And an eternal curse fall on you! Let me know.
Why sinks that cauldron? and what noise is this?
[*Hautboys.*
FIRST WITCH. Show!
SEC. WITCH. Show!
THIRD WITCH. Show!
ALL. Show his eyes, and grieve his heart;
Come like shadows, so depart!

[*A show of Eight* KINGS, *the last with a glass in his hand;* BANQUO'S GHOST *following.*]

MACB. Thou are too like the spirit of Banquo; down!
Thy crown does sear mine eye-balls. And thy hair,
Thou other gold-bound brow, is like the first.
A third is like the former. Filthy hags!
Why do you show me this? A fourth! Start, eyes!
What, will the line stretch out to the crack of doom?
Another yet! A seventh! I'll see no more:
And yet the eighth appears, who bears a glass
Which shows me many more; and some I see
That two-fold balls and treble sceptres carry:
Horrible sight! Now, I see, 'tis true;
For the blood-bolter'd Banquo smiles upon me,
And points at them for his. [APPARITIONS *vanish.*] What, is this so?
FIRST WITCH. Ay, sir, all this is so: but why
Stands Macbeth thus amazedly?

106. noise, music. **s.d. Eight Kings,** eight Scottish Kings, the last of whom is James I of England, all descendants of Banquo. **112. down,** disappear. **116. Start, eyes,** i.e., I feel my eyes bulge (with horror). **117. crack or doom,** sound made by the rending of the earth when the graves are torn open on the day of Judgment. **121. two-fold balls,** insignia of sovereignty over England and Scotland; **treble sceptres,** a reference to King James's title, "King of Great Britain, France and Ireland." **123. blood-bolter'd,** clotted with blood.

Come, sisters, cheer we up his sprites,
And show the best of our delights:
I'll charm the air to give a sound,
While you perform your antic round;
That this great king may kindly say,
Our duties did his welcome pay.
[*Music. The* WITCHES *dance, and then vanish, with* HECATE.

MACB. Where are they? Gone? Let this pernicious hour
Stand aye accursèd in the calendar!
Come in, without there!

[*Enter* LENNOX.]

LEN. What's your grace's will?
MACB. Saw you the weird sisters?
LEN. No, my lord.
MACB. Came they not by you?
LEN. No, indeed, my lord.
MACB. Infected be the air whereon they ride;
And damn'd all those that trust them! I did hear
The galloping of horse: who was 't came by?
LEN. 'Tis two or three, my lord, that bring you word
Macduff is fled to England.
MACB. Fled to England!
LEN. Ay, my good lord.
MACB. Time, thou anticipatest my dread expolits:
The flighty purpose never is o'ertook
Unless the deed go with it: from this moment
The very firstlings of my heart shall be
The firstlings of my hand. And even now,
To crown my thoughts with acts, be it thought and done:
The castle of Macduff I will surprise;
Seize upon Fife; give to the edge o' the sword

130. antic round, grotesque dance in a circle. **144. anticipatest,** forestall. **145. flighty,** fleeting. **147. firstling,** first born.

His wife, his babes, and all unfortunate souls
That trace him in his line. No boasting like a fool:
This deed I'll do before this purpose cool.
But no more sights!—Where are these gentlemen?
Come, bring me where they are. [*Exeunt.*

SCENE II. *Fife.* MACDUFF'S *castle.*

[*Enter* LADY MACDUFF, *her* SON, *and* ROSS.]

L. MACD. What had he done, to make him fly the land?
ROSS. You must have patience, madam.
L. MACD. He had none:
His flight was madness: when our actions do not,
Our fears do make us traitors.
ROSS. You know not
Whether it was his wisdom or his fear.
L. MACD. Wisdom! to leave his wife, to leave his babes,
His mansion and his titles in a place
From whence himself does fly? He loves us not;
He wants the natural touch: for the poor wren,
The most diminutive of birds, will fight,
Her young ones in her nest, against the owl.
All is the fear and nothing is the love;
As little is the wisdom, where the flight
So runs against all reason.
ROSS. My dearest coz,
I pray you, school yourself: but for your husband,
He is noble, wise, judicious, and best knows
The fits o' the season. I dare not speak much further;
But cruel are the times, when we are traitors
And do not know ourselves, when we hold rumour
From what we fear, yet know not what we fear,

153. trace . . . line, i.e., of his lineage or blood relatives. **Scene ii: 2. patience,** self-control. **7. titles,** estates. **9. natural touch,** instincts of affection. **15. for,** as for. **17. fits . . . season,** crises of the time. **18. are traitors,** are accused of being traitors. **19. know ourselves,** i.e., to be traitors; **hold,** accept. **20. From,** because of.

But float upon a wild and violent sea
Each way and move. I take my leave of you:
Shall not be long but I'll be here again:
Things at the worst will cease, or else climb upward
To what they were before. My pretty cousin,
Blessing upon you!
L. MACD. Father'd he is, and yet he's fatherless.
ROSS. I am so much a fool, should I stay longer,
It would be my disgrace and your discomfort:
I take my leave at once. [*Exit.*
L. MACD. Sirrah, your father's dead:
And what will you do now? How will you live?
SON. As birds do, mother.
L. MACD. What, with worms and flies?
SON. With what I get, I mean; and so do they.
L. MACD. Poor bird! thou'ldst never fear the net nor lime,
The pitfall nor the gin.
SON. Why should I, mother? Poor birds they are not set for.
My father is not dead, for all your saying.
L. MACD. Yes, he is dead: how wilt thou do for a father?
SON. Nay, how will you do for a husband?
L. MACD. Why, I can buy me twenty at any market.
SON. Then you'll buy 'em to sell again.
L. MACD. Thou speak'st with all thy wit; and yet, i' faith,
With wit enough for thee.
SON. Was my father a traitor, mother?
L. MACD. Ay, that he was.
SON. What is a traitor?
L. MACD. Why, one that swears and lies.
SON. And be all traitors that do so?

22. Each . . . move, in every direction. **29. It . . . disgrace,** i.e., I should weep. **34. lime,** a sticky substance spread on the boughs of trees to catch birds. **35. pitfall,** trap; **gin,** snare. **36. Poor . . . set for,** i.e., traps are not set for poor birds (like me). **41. sell,** (1) to vend, (2) to deceive. **42. Thou . . . wit,** i.e., you are only as intelligent as a child can be. **47. swears and lies,** takes an oath (of allegiance)

L. MACD. Every one that does so is a traitor, and must be hanged.

SON. And must they all be hanged that swear and lie?

L. MACD. Every one.

SON. Who must hang them?

L. MACD. Why, the honest men.

SON. Then the liars and swearers are fools, for there are liars and swearers enow to beat the honest men and hang up them.

L. MACD. Now, God help thee, poor monkey! But how wilt thou do for a father?

SON. If he were dead, you'ld weep for him: if you would not, it were a good sign that I should quickly have a new father.

L. MACD. Poor prattler, how thou talk'st!

[*Enter a* MESSENGER.]

MESS. Bless you, fair dame! I am not to you known,
Though in your state of honour I am perfect. I doubt some
danger does approach you nearly;
If you will take a homely man's advice,
Be not found here; hence, with your little ones.
To fright you thus, methinks, I am too savage;
To do worse to you were fell cruelty,
Which is too nigh your person. Heaven preserve you!
I dare abide no longer. [*Exit.*

L. MACD. Wither should I fly?
I have done no harm. But I remember now
I am in this earthly world; where to do harm
Is often laudable, to do good sometime
Accounted dangerous folly: why then, alas,
Do I put up that womanly defence,
To say I have done no harm?

and breaks it. **57. enow,** enough. **66. in . . . perfect,** I well know you are honorable. **67. doubt,** suspect. **68. homely,** humble. **71. To do worse,** i.e., to frighten you more.

[*Enter* MURDERERS.]

What are these faces?
FIRST MUR. Where is your husband?
L. MACD. I hope, in no place so unsanctified
Whert such as thou mayst find him.
FIRST MUR. He's a traitor.
SON. Thou liest, thou shag-hair'd villian!
FIRST MUR. What, you egg!
[*Stabbing him.*]
Young fry of treachery!
SON. He has kill'd me, mother:
Run away, I pray you! [*Dies.*
[*Exit* LADY MACDUFF, *crying* "Murder!"
Exeunt MURDERERS, *following her.*]

SCENE III. *England. Before the King's palace.*

[*Enter* MALCOLM *and* MACDUFF.]

MAL. Let us seek out some desolate shade and there
Weep our sad bosoms empty.
MACD. Let us rather
Hold fast the mortal sword, and like good men
Bestride our down-fall'n birthdom: each new morn
New widows howl, new orphans cry, new sorrows
Strike heaven on the face, that it resounds
As if it felt with Scotland and yell'd out
Like syllable of dolour.
MAL. What I believe I'll wail,
What know believe, and what I can redress,
As I shall find the time to friend, I will.
What you have spoke, it may be so perchance.

83. shag-hair'd, having shaggy hair hanging about the ears; **egg,** unhatched (traitor). **84. fry of treachery,** child of a traitor. **Scene iii: 3. mortal,** deadly. **4. Bestride,** stand over as defenders; **birthdom,** native land. **6. that,** so that. **8. Like . . . dolour,** like a similar cry of grief. **10. time to friend,** favorable opportunity. **12. sole,** mere. **13.**

This tryant, whose sole name blisters our tongues,
Was once thought honest: you have loved him well;
He hath not touch'd you yet. I am young; but something
You may deserve of him through me, and wisdom
To offer up a weak poor innocent lamb
To appease an angry god.

MACD. I am not treacherous.

MAL. But Macbeth is.
A good and virtuous nature may recoil
In an imperial charge. But I shall crave your pardon;
That which you are my thoughts cannot transpose:
Angels are bright still, though the brightest fell:
Though all things foul would wear the brows of grace,
Yet grace must still look so.

MACD. I have lost my hopes.

MAL. Perchance even there where I did find my doubts.
Why in that rawness left you wife and child,
Those precious motives, those strong knots of love,
Without leave-taking? I pray you,
Let not my jealousies be your dishonours,
But mine own safeties. You may be rightly just,
Whatever I shall think.

MACD. Bleed, bleed, poor country!
Great tyranny! lay thou thy basis sure,
For goodness dare not check thee: wear thou thy wrongs;
The title is affeer'd! Fare thee well, lord:
I would not be the villain that thou think'st
For the whole space that's in the tyrant's grasp,

honest, upright. **15. deserve . . . me,** gain a reward from him by betraying me; **wisdom,** it would be wise. **19-20. may . . . charge,** may (like a spring) yield under pressure of a royal command. **21. transpose,** change. **23. would . . . grace,** should try to wear the appearance of virtue. **24. look so,** appear virtuous; **hopes,** i.e., of persuading you to lead the revolt against Macbeth. **25. doubts,** of your honor. **26. rawness,** unprotected state. **27. motives,** i.e., to action. **29-30. Let . . . safeties,** regard my suspicions not as dishonoring you, but as protecting myself. **33. thy wrongs,** what you have wrongfully gained. **34. affeer'd,** confirmed (since Malcolm will not act).

And the rich East to boot.
MAL. Be not offended:
I speak not as in absolute fear of you.
I think our country sinks beneath the yoke;
It weeps, it bleeds; and each new day a gash
Is added to her wounds: I think withal
There would be hands uplifted in my right;
And here from gracious England have I offer
Of goodly thousands: but, for all this,
When I shall tread upon the tyrant's head,
Or wear it on my sword, yet my poor country
Shall have more vices than it had before,
More suffer and more sundry ways then ever,
By him that shall succeed.
MACD. What should he be?
MAL. It is myself I mean: in whom I know
All the particulars of vice so grafted
That, when they shall be open'd, black Macbeth
Will seem as pure as snow, and the poor state
Esteem him as a lamb, being compared
With my confineless harms.
MACD. Not in the legions
Of horrid hell can come a devil more damn'd
In evils to top Macbeth.
MAL. I grant him bloody,
Luxurious, avaricious, false, deceitful,
Sudden, malicious, smacking of every sin
That has a name: but there's no bottom, none,
In my voluptuousness: your wives, your daughters,
Your matrons and your maids, could not fill up
The cistern of my lust, and my desire
All continent impediments would o'erbear

38. I speak . . . you, i.e., I am not entirely convinced of your intentions toward me. **41, withal,** besides. **43. England,** the King of England. **49. What . . . be?** Who can that be? **51. grafted,** engrafted. **52. open'd,** i.e., like buds grafted on the stem of another plant. **55. confineless harms,** boundless injuries (I might do). **58. Luxurious,** licentious.

That did oppose my will: better Macbeth
Than such an one to reign.

MACD. Boundless intemperance
In nature is a tyranny; it hath been
The untimely emptying of the happy throne
And fall of many kings. But fear not yet
To take upon you what is yours: you may
Convey your pleasures in a spacious plenty,
And yet seem cold, the time you may so hoodwink.
We have willing dames enough; there cannot be
That vulture in you, to devour so many
As will to greatness dedicate themselves,
Finding it so inclined.

MAL. With this there grows
In my most ill-composed affection such
A stanchless avarice that, were I king,
I should cut off the nobles for their lands,
Desire his jewels and this other's house:
And my more-having would be as a sauce
To make me hunger more; that I should forge
Quarrels unjust against the good and loyal,
Destroying them for wealth.

MACD. This avarice
Sticks deeper, grows with more pernicious root
Than summer-seeming lust, and it hath been
The sword of our slain kings: yet do not fear;
Scotland hath foisons to fill up your will,
Of your mere own: all these are portable,
With other graces weigh'd.

59. **Sudden.** violent. 64. **continent,** restraining; **o'erbear,** overpower. 67. **In . . . tyranny,** tyrannizes over the other elements of man's nature. 69. **yet,** however. 71. **Convey,** obtain secretly. 72. **cold,** chaste; **time . . . hoodwink,** so deceive the age. 77. **ill-composed affection,** my disposition composed of evil elements. 82. **that,** with the result that. 86. **summer-seeming,** short and feverish (like summer). 87. **sword . . . kings,** cause of the death of our kings who have been slain. 88. **foisons,** plentiful stores; **will,** greedy lust. 89. **mere own,** very own possessions; **portable,** endurable. 90. **weigh'd,** balanced. 92. **verity,** honesty.

MAL. But I have none: the king-becoming graces,
As justice, verity, temperance, stableness,
Bounty, perseverance, mercy, lowliness,
Devotion, patience, courage, fortitude,
I have no relish of them, but abound
In the division of each several crime,
Acting it many ways. Nay, had I power I should
Pour the sweet milk of concord into hell,
Uproar the universal peace, confound
All unity on earth.
MACD. O Scotland, Scotland!
MAL. If such a one be fit to govern, speak:
I am as I have spoken.
MACD. Fit to govern!
No, not to live. O nation miserable,
With an untitled tyrant bloody-scepter'd,
When shalt thou see thy wholesome days again,
Since that the truest issue of thy throne
By his own interdiction stands accursed,
And does blaspheme his breed? Thy royal father
Was a most sainted king: the queen that bore thee,
Oftener upon her knees than on her feet,
Died every day she lived. Fare thee well!
These evils thou repeat'st upon thyself
Have banish'd me from Scotland. O my breast,
Thy hope ends here!
MAL. Macduff, this noble passion,
Child of integrity, hath from my soul
Wiped the black scruples, reconciled my thoughts
To thy good truth and honour. Devilish Macbeth
By many of these trains hath sought to win me

93. **Bounty,** generosity. 95. **relish,** trace. 96. **In the division,** in every variation. 99. **confound,** destroy. 104. **untitled tyrant,** tyrannical usurper. 106. **truest issue,** nearest heir. 107. **By . . . interdiction,** by debarring himself. 108. **blaspheme,** slander. 111. **Died,** i.e., unto the world, renounced it, cf. I Corinthians XV:31 "I protest by your rejoicing which I have in Jesus Christ our Lord, I die daily." 112. **repeat'st upon,** enumerated against.

Into his power, and modest wisdom plucks me
From over-credulous haste: but God above
Deal between thee and me! for even now
I put myself to thy direction, and
Unspeak mine own detraction, here abjure
The taints and blames I laid upon myself,
For strangers to my nature. I am yet
Unknown to woman, never was forsworn,
Scarcely have coveted what was mine own,
At no time broke my faith, would not betray
The devil to his fellow, and delight
No less in truth than life: my first false speaking
Was this upon myself: what I am truly,
Is thine and my poor country's to command:
Whither indeed, before thy here-approach,
Old Siward, with ten thousand warlike men,
Already at a point, was setting forth.
Now we'll together; and the chance of goodness
Be like our warranted quarrel! Why are you silent?

MACD. Such welcome and unwelcome things at once
'Tis hard to reconcile.

[*Enter a* DOCTOR.]

MAL. Well; more anon.—Comes the king forth, I pray you?

DOCT. Ay, sir; there are a crew of wretched souls
That stay his cure: their malady convinces
The great assay of art; but at his touch—
Such sanctity hath heaven given his hand—
They presently amend.

MAL. I thank you, doctor. [*Exit* DOCTOR.

118. **trains,** tricks. 119. **modest,** sober. 121. **Deal . . . me,** i.e., keep our friendship safe. 123. **Unspeak . . . detraction,** take back the charges I have made against myself. 133. **Whither,** i.e., toward my country. 135. **at a point,** fully armed. 136. **goodness,** success. 137, **like . . . quarrel,** as good as the justice of our cause. 142. **stay his cure,** wait for him to cure them; **convinces,** baffles. 143. **The . . . art,** the

MACD. What's the disease he means?
MAL. 'Tis call'd the evil:
A most miraculous work in this good king;
Which often, since my here-remain in England,
I have seen him do. How he solicits heaven,
Himself best knows: but strangely-visited people,
All swoln and ulcerous, pitiful to the eye,
The mere despair of surgery, he cures,
Hanging a golden stamp about their necks,
Put on with holy prayers: and 'tis spoken,
To the succeeding royalty he leaves
The healing benediction. With this strange virtue,
He hath a heavenly gift of prophecy,
And sundry blessings hang about his throne,
That speak him full of grace.

[*Enter* ROSS.]

MACD. See, who comes here?
MAL. My countryman; but yet I know him not.
MACD. My ever-gentle cousin, welcome hither.
MAL. I know him now. Good God, betimes remove
The means that makes us strangers!
ROSS. Sir, amen.
MACD. Stands Scotland where it did?
ROSS. Alas, poor country!
Almost afraid to know itself. It cannot
Be call'd our mother, but our grave; where nothing,
But who knows nothing, is once seen to smile;
Where sighs and groans and shrieks that rend the air
Are made, not mark'd; where violent sorrow seems
A modern ecstasy: the dead man's knell

greatest efforts of medicine. **145. presently amend,** immediately recover. **146. the evil,** the King's evil, i.e., scrofula or tuberculosis of the skin. **150. strangely,** with strange diseases. **152. mere,** complete. **153. stamp,** coin. **154. spoken,** said. **156. With,** in addition to; **virtue,** power. **159. grace,** holiness. **163. The means,** Macbeth. **166. nothing,** no one. **170. modern ecstasy,** an everyday emotion.

Is there scarce ask'd for who; and good men's lives
Expire before the flowers in their caps,
Dying or ere they sicken.
MACD. O, relation
Too nice, and yet too true!
MAL. What's the newest grief?
ROSS. That of an hour's age doth hiss the speaker:
Each minute teems a new one.
MACD. How does my wife?
ROSS. Why, well.
MACD. And all my children?
ROSS. Well too.
MACD. The tyrant has not batter'd at their peace?
ROSS. No; they were well at peace when I did leave 'em.
MACD. Be not a niggard of your speech: how goes 't?
ROSS. When I came hither to transport the tidings,
Which I have heavily borne, there ran a rumour
Of many worthy fellows that were out;
Which was to my belief witness'd the rather,
For that I saw the tyrant's power a-foot:
Now is the time of help; your eye in Scotland
Would create soldiers, make our women fight,
To doff their dire distresses.
MAL. Be 't their comfort
We are coming thither: gracious England hath
Lent us good Siward and ten thousand men;
An older and a better soldier none
That Christendom gives out.
ROSS. Would I could answer
This comfort with the like! But I have words
That would be howl'd out in the desert air,
Where hearing should not latch them.

173-4. relation Too nice, narrative too exact. **175. hiss the speaker,** i.e., because his news is already stale. **176. teems,** gives birth to. **182. heavily,** sorrowfully. **183. out,** under arms, i.e., in rebellion. **184. Which . . . rather,** which I the more readily believed. **185. power,** army. **186. your eye,** the sight of you. **188. doff,** put off. **192. gives out,** tells of. **195. latch,** catch.

MACD. What concern they?
The general cause? or is it a fee-grief
Due to some single breast?
ROSS. No mind that's honest
But in it shares some woe; though the main part
Pertains to you alone.
MACD. If it be mine,
Keep it not from me, quickly let me have it.
ROSS. Let not your ears despise my tongue for ever,
Which shall possess them with the heaviest sound
That ever yet they heard.
MACD. Hum! I guess at it.
ROSS. Your castle is surprised; your wife and babes
Savagely slaughter'd: to relate the manner,
Were, on the quarry of these murder'd deer,
To add the death of you.
MAL. Merciful heaven!
What, man! ne'er pull your hat upon your brows;
Give sorrow words: the grief that does not speak
Whispers the o'er-fraught heart and bids it break.
MACD. My children too?
ROSS. Wife, children, servants, all
That could be found.
MACD. And I must be from thence!
My wife kill'd too?
ROSS. I have said.
MAL. Be comforted:
Let's make us medicines of our great revenge,
To cure this deadly grief.
MACD. He has no children. All my pretty ones?
Did you say all? O hell-kite! All?
What, all my pretty chickens and their dam
At one fell swoop?
MAL. Dispute it like a man.

196. fee-grief, private grief. **197. honest,** well-intentioned. **202. heaviest,** saddest. **206. quarry,** heap of slaughtered game. **210. o'er-fraught,**

MACD. I shall do so;
But I must also feel it as a man:
I cannot but remember such things were,
That were most precious to me. Did heaven look on,
And would not take their part? Sinful Macduff,
They were all struck for thee! naught that I am,
Not for their own demerits, but for mine,
Fell slaughter on their souls. Heaven rest them now!

MAL. Be this the whetstone of your sword: let grief
Convert to anger; blunt not the heart, enrage it.

MACD. O, I could play the woman with mine eyes
And braggart with my tongue! But, gentle heavens,
Cut short all intermission; front to front
Bring thou this fiend of Scotland and myself;
Within my sword's length set him; if he 'scape,
Heaven forgive him too!

MAL. This tune goes manly.
Come, go we to the king; our power is ready;
Our lack is nothing but our leave: Macbeth
Is ripe for shaking, and the powers above
Put on their instruments. Receive what cheer you may:
The night is long that never finds the day.
[*Exeunt.*

ACT V

SCENE I. *Dunsinane. Ante-room in the castle.*

[*Enter a* DOCTOR OF PHYSIC *and a* WAITING-GENTLEWOMAN.]

DOCT. I have two nights watched with you, but can perceive no truth in your report. When was it she last walked?

overladen. **212. And . . . thence!** And I had to be away! **220. Dispute it,** take action against it (this outrage). **225. naught,** wicked man. **229. Convert,** change. **230. I . . . eyes,** i.e., I could weep. **231. braggart . . . tongue,** express my grief extravagantly. **232. intermission,** delay. **237. lack . . . leave,** all that we lack is the permission to leave England. **239. Put . . . instruments,** urge on their agents; **cheer,** fare. **Act V,**

GENT. Since his majesty went into the field, I have seen her rise from her bed, throw her nightgown upon her, unlock her closet, take forth paper, fold it, write upon 't, read it, afterwards seal it, and again return to bed; yet all this while in a most fast sleep.

DOCT. A great perturbation in nature, to receive at once the benefit of sleep, and do the effects of watching! In this slumbery agitation, besides her walking and other actual performances, what, at any time, have you heard her say!

GENT. That, sir, which I will not report after her.

DOCT. You may to me: and 'tis most meet you should.

GENT. Neither to you nor any one, having no witness to confirm my speech.

[*Enter* LADY MACBETH, *with a taper.*]

Lo you, here she comes! This is her very guise; and, upon my life, fast asleep. Observe her; stand close.

DOCT. How came she by that light?

GENT. Why, it stood by her? she has light by her continually; 'tis her command.

DOCT. You see, her eyes are open.

GENT. Ay, but their sense is shut.

DOCT. What is it she does now? Look, how she rubs her hands.

GENT. It is an accustomed action with her, to seem thus washing her hands; I have known her continue in this a quarter of an hour.

LADY M. Yet here's a spot.

DOCT. Hark! she speaks: I will set down what comes from her, to satisfy my remembrance the more strongly.

LADY M. Out, damned spot! out, I say!—One: two: why,

Scene i: 7. closet, cabinet. **11-2. do . . . watching,** act as though she were awake. **13. agitation,** activity. **22-3. her very guise,** is exactly the way she looks (when walking in her sleep). **24. close,** out of sight. **29. sense,** ability to see. **35. Yet . . . spot,** there's still a spot here. **37. satisfy,** assure.

then 'tis time to do 't.—Hell is murky!—Fie, my lord, fie! a soldier, and afeard? What need we fear who knows it, when none can call our power to account?—Yet who would have thought the old man to have had so much blood in him.

DOCT. Do you mark that?

LADY M. The thane of Fife had a wife: where is she now? —What, will these hands nee'r be clean?—No more o' that, my lord, no more o' that: you mar all with this starting.

DOCT. Go to, go to; you known what you should not.

GENT. She has spoke what she should not, I am sure of that: heaven knows what she has known.

LADY M. Here's the smell of the blood still: all the perfumes of Arabia will not sweeten this little hand. Oh, oh, oh!

DOCT. What a sigh is there? The heart is sorely charged.

GENT. I would not have such a heart in my bosom for the dignity of the whole body.

DOCT. Well, well, well,—

GENT. Pray God it be, sir.

DOCT. This disease is beyond my practice; yet I have known those which have walked in their sleep who have died holily in their beds.

LADY M. Wash your hands, put on your nightgown; look not so pale.—I tell you yet again, Banquo's buried; he cannot come out on 's grave.

DOCT. Even so?

LADY M. To bed, to bed! there's knocking at the gate: come, come, come, come, give me your hand. What's done cannot be undone.—To bed, to bed, to bed!

[*Exit.*

DOCT. Will she go now to bed?

GENT. Directly.

DOCT. Foul whisperings are abroad: unnatural deeds
Do breed unnatural troubles: infected minds

51. **Go to, go to,** about="dear, dear." **60. charged,** burdened. **62. for . . . body,** in return for all her royal dignity. **65. practice,** skill.

To their deaf pillows will discharge their secrets:
More needs she the divine than the physician.
God, God, forgive us all! Look after her;
Remove from her the means of all annoyance,
And still keep eyes upon her. So, good night:
My mind she has mated, and amazed my sight.
I think, but dare not speak.

GENT. Good night, good doctor.

[*Exeunt.*

SCENE II. *The country near Dunsinane.*

[*Drum and colours. Enter* MENTEITH, CAITHNESS, ANGUS, LENNOX, *and* SOLDIERS.]

MENT. The English power is near, led on by Malcolm,
His uncle Siward and the good Macduff:
Revenges burn in them; for their dear causes
Would to the bleeding and the grim alarm
Excite the mortified man.

ANG. Near Birnam wood
Shall we well meet them; that way are they coming.

CAITH. Who knows if Donalbain be with his brother?

LEN. For certain, sir, he is not: I have a file
Of all the gentry: there is Siward's son,
And many unrough youths that even now
Protest their first of manhood.

MENT. What does the tyrant?

CAITH. Great Dunsinane he strongly fortifies:
Some say he's mad: others that lesser hate him
Do call it valiant fury: but, for certain,
He cannot buckle his distemper'd cause

84. annoyance, self-injury. **86. mated,** dazed. **Scene ii: 3. dear causes,** deeply felt grievances. **4-5. Would . . . man,** would excite even a paralytic to a bloody and grim attack. **6. well,** probably. **8. file,** list. **10. unrough,** beardless. **11. Protest . . . manhood,** give first evidence of their manhood. **15. distemper'd cause,** sick (perverse) course of action. **16. Within . . . rule,** i.e., by measures of rational conduct. The figure is that of buckling in a swollen stomach.

Within the belt of rule.

ANG. Now does he feel
His secret murders sticking on his hands;
Now minutely revolts upbraid his faith-breach;
Those he commands move only in command,
Nothing in love; now does he feel his title
Hang loose about him, like a giant's robe
Upon a dwarfish thief.

MENT. Who then shall blame
His pester'd senses to recoil and start,
When all that is within him does condemn
Itself for being there?

CAITH. Well, march we on,
To give obedience where 'tis truly owed:
Meet we the medicine of the sickly weal,
And with him pour we in our country's purge
Each drop of us.

LEN. Or so much as it needs,
To dew the sovereign flower and drown the weeds.
Make we our march towards Birnam.

[*Exeunt, marching.*

SCENE III. *Dunsinane. A room in the castle.*

[*Enter* MACBETH, DOCTOR, *and* ATTENDANTS.]

MACB. Bring me no more reports; let them fly all:
Till Birnam wood remove to Dunsinane,
I cannot taint with fear. What's the boy Malcolm?
Was he not born of woman? The spirits that know
All mortal consequences have pronounced me thus:
"Fear not Macbeth; no man that's born of woman
Shal e'er have power upon thee." Then fly, false thanes,

18. minutely . . . faith-breach, the revoits occurring every minute are a reproof of his own breach of faith. **19. more . . . command,** act only because they are under military orders. **23. pester'd senses,** harassed mind. **27. medicine,** i.e., Malcolm; **weal,** realm. **30. sovereign flower,** i.e., Malcolm. **Scene iii: 1. them,** his nobles. **3. taint,** be infected. **5. mortal consequences,** human destinies.

And mingle with the English epicures:
The mind I sway by and the heart I bear
Shall never sag with doubt nor shake with fear.

[*Enter a* SERVANT.]

The devil damn thee black, thou cream-faced loon!
Where got'st thou that goose look?
SERV. There is ten thousand—
MACB. Geese, villain?
SERV. Soldiers, sir.
MACB. Go, prick they face, and over-red thy fear,
Thou lily-liver'd boy. What soldiers, patch?
Death of thy soul! those linen cheeks of thine
Are counsellors to fear. What soldiers, why-face?
SERV. The English force, so please you.
MACB. Take thy face hence. [Exit SERVANT.]
Seyton!—I am sick at heart,
When I behold—Seyton, I say!—This push
Will cheer me ever, or disseat me now.
I have lived long enough: my way of life
Is fall'n into the sear, the yellow leaf;
And that which should accompany old age,
As honour, love, obedience troops of friends,
I must not look to have; but, in their stead,
Curses, not loud but deep, mouth-honour, breath,
Which the poor heart would fain deny, and dare not.
Seyton!

[*Enter* SEYTON.]

SEY. What is your gracious pleasure?
MACB. What news more?
SEY. All is confirm'd, my lord, which was reported.
MACB. I'll fight till from my bones my flesh be hack'd

9. **I sway by,** depend on. 14. **over-red,** redden all over (with blood). 15. **patch,** fool. 17. **Are . . . fear,** inspire fear (in others). 20. **push,** emergency. 21. **disseat,** dethrone. 23. **sear,** withered.

Give me my armour.
SEY. 'Tis not needed yet.
MACB. I'll put it on.
Send out moe horses; skirr the country round;
Hang those that talk of fear. Give me mine armour.
How does your patient, doctor?
DOCT. Not so sick, my lord,
As she is troubled with thick-coming fancies,
That keep her from her rest.
MACB. Cure her of that.
Canst thou not minister to a mind diseased,
Pluck from the memory a rooted sorrow,
Raze out the written troubles of the brain
And with some sweet oblivious antidote
Cleanse the stuff'd bosom of that perilous stuff
Which weighs upon the heart?
DOCT. Therein the patient
Must minister to himself.
MACB. Throw physic to the dogs; I'll none of it.
Come, pit mine armour on; give me my staff.
Seyton, send out. Doctor, the thanes fly from me.
Come, sir, dispatch. If thou couldst, doctor, cast
The water of my land, find her disease,
And purge it to a sound and pristine health,
I would applaud thee to the very echo,
That should applaud again.—Pull 't off, I say.—
What rhubarb, senna, or what purgative drug,
Would scour these English hence? Hear'st thou of them?
DOCT. Ay, my good lord; your royal preparation
Makes us hear something.
MACB. Bring it after me.

35. **moe horses,** more horsemen; **skirr . . . round,** scurry about the country. 42. **Raze out,** scratch out. 43. **oblivious,** causing forgetfulness. 44. **stuff'd,** overburdened. 47. **physic,** medicine (of any sort). 48. **staff,** lance. 50-1. **cast The water,** analyze the urine, then a common method of medicine diagnosis. 52. **sound . . . health,** original sound health. 54. **Pull't off,** i.e., some piece of this armor.

I will not be afraid of death and bane,
Till Birnam forest come to Dunsinane.
DOCT. [*Aside*] Were I from Dunsinane away and clear,
Profit again should hardly draw me here. [*Exeunt.*

SCENE IV. *Country near Birnam wood.*

[*Drum and colours. Enter* MALCOLM, *old* SIWARD *and his* SON, MACDUFF, MENTEITH, CAITHNESS, ANGUS, LENNOX, ROSS, *and* SOLDIERS, *marching.*]

MAL. Cousins, I hope the days are near at hand
That chambers will be safe.
MENT. We doubt it nothing.
SIW. What wood is this before us?
MENT. The wood of Birnam.
MAL. Let every soldier hew him down a bough
And bear't before him: thereby shall we shadow
The numbers of our host and make discovery
Err in report of us.
SOLDIERS. It shall be done.
SIW. We learn no other but the confident tyrant
Keeps still in Dunsinane, and will endure
Our setting down before 't.
MAL. 'Tis his main hope:
For where there is advantage to be given,
Both more and less have given him the revolt,
And none serve with him but constrainèd things
Whose hearts are absent too.
MACD. Let our just censures
Attend the true event, and put we on

56. scour . . . hence, clear . . . out. **58. Makes . . . something,** tells us something about (their advance). **Scene iv: 2. chambers,** bedchambers. **5. shadow,** conceal. **6. discovery,** i.e., Macbeth's patrols. **8. We . . . but,** our only information is that. **9. Keeps still,** continues to remain. **10. setting . . . befor 't,** laying siege to it. **11. advantage,** opportunity. **12. more and less,** men of both high and low rank. **13. constrained things,** poor coerced creatures. **14. just censures,** correct judgment (of Macbeth's army). **15. Attend . . . event,** await the final outcome (of

Industrious soldiership.

SIW. The time approaches
That will with due decision make us know
What we shall say we have and what we owe.
Thoughts speculative their unsure hopes relate,
But certain issue strokes must arbitrate:
Towards which advance the war.

[*Exeunt, marching.*

SCENE V. *Dunsinane. Within the castle.*

[*Enter* MACBETH, SEYTON, *and* SOLDIERS, *with drum and colours.*]

MACB. Hang out our banners on the outward walls:
The cry is still "They come:" our castle's strength
Will laugh a siege to scorn: here let them lie
Till famine and the ague eat them up:
Were they not forced with those that should be ours,
We might have met them dareful, beard to beard,
And beat them backward home.

[*A cry of women within.*]

What is that noise?

SEY. It is the cry of women, my good lord.

[*Exit.*

MACB. I have almost forgot the taste of fears:
The time has been, my senses would have cool'd
To hear a night-shriek; and my fell of hair
Would at a dismal treatise rouse and stir
As life were in 't: I have supp'd full with horrors;
Direness, familiar to my slaughterous thoughts,
Cannot once start me.

[*Re-enter* SEYTON.]

the battle). **18. What . . . owe,** what we merely claim to have and what we actually hold. **19. Thoughts . . . relate,** wishful thinking merely reveals one's uncertain hope. **20. certain . . . arbitrate,** strokes (of the sword) must determine the final outcome. **21. which,** i.e., the outcome. **Scene v: 4. vague,** fever. **5. forced,** reinforced. **10. cool'd,** shivered

Wherefore was that cry?
SEY. The queen, my lord, is dead.
MACB. She should have died hereafter;
There would have been a time for such a word.
To-morrow, and to-morrow, and to-morrow,
Creeps in this petty pace from day to day
To the last syllable of recorded time,
And all our yesterdays have lighted fools
The way to dusty death. Out, out, brief candle!
Life's but a walking shadow, a poor player
That struts and frets his hour upon the stage
And then is heard no more: it is a tale
Told by an idiot, full of sound and fury,
Signifying nothing.

[*Enter a* MESSENGER.]

Thou comest to use thy tongue; thy story quickly.
MESS. Gracious my lord,
I should report that which I say I saw,
But know not how to do it.
MACB. Well, say, sir.
MESS. As I did stand my watch upon the hill,
I look'd toward Birnam, and anon, methought,
The wood began to move.
MACB. Liar and slave!
MESS. Let me endure your wrath, if 't be not so:
Within this three mile may you see it coming;
I say, a moving grove.
MACB. If thou speak'st false,
Upon the next tree shalt thou hang alive,
Till famine cling thee: if thy speech be sooth,
I care not if thou dost for me as much.

(with terror). **11. fell of hair,** all the hair on my body. **12. treatise,** tale. **13. As,** As if. **15. start,** startle. **17. should . . . hereafter,** would have died some time in the future, i.e., she had to die sometime. **18. word,** i.e., death. **34. anon,** all at once. **40. cling,** shrivel; **sooth,** truth.

I pull in resolution, and begin
To doubt the equivocation of the fiend
That lies like truth: "Fear not, till Birnam wood
Do come to Dunsinane:" and now a wood
Comes toward Dunsinane. Arm, arm , and out!
If this which he avouches does appear,
There is nor flying hence nor tarrying here.
I 'gin to be aweary of the sun,
And wish the estate o' the world were now undone.
Ring the alarum-bell! Blow, wind! come, wrack!
At least we'll die with harness on our back.

[*Exeunt.*

SCENE VI. *Dunsinane. Before the castle.*

[*Drum and colours. Enter* MALCOLM, *old* SIWARD, MACDUFF, *and their Army with boughs.*]

MAL. Now near enough: your leavy screens throw down,
And show like those you are. You, worthy uncle,
Shall, with my cousin, your right-noble son,
Lead our first battle: worthy Macduff and we
Shall take upon's what else remains to do,
According to our order.

SIW. Fare you well.
Do we but find the tyrant's power to-night,
Let us be beaten, if we cannot fight.

MACD. Make all our trumpets speak; give them all breath,
Those clamorous harbingers of blood and death. [*Exeunt.*

SCENE VII. *Another part of the field.*

[*Alarums. Enter* MACBETH.]

MACB. They have tied me to a stake; I cannot fly,
But, bear-like, I must fight the course. What's he

42. pull in resolution, rein in my confidence. **50. estate o' the world,** order of the universe. **51. wrack,** ruin. **52. harness,** armor. **Scene vi: 4. battle,** division. **6. order,** plan. **Scene vii: 2. course,** one bout in the sport of bear-baiting.

That was not born of woman? Such a one
Am I to fear, or none.

[*Enter young* SIWARD.]

YO. SIW. What is thy name?
MACB. Thou'lt be afraid to hear it.
YO. SIW. No; though thou call'st thyself a hotter name
Than any is in hell.
MACB. My name's Macbeth.
YO. SIW. The devil himself could not pronounce a title
More hateful to mine ear.
MACB. No, nor more fearful.
YO. SIW. Thou liest, abhorrèd tyrant; with my sword
I'll prove the lie thou speak'st
[*They fight and young* SIWARD *is slain.*
MACB. Thou wast born of woman.
But swords I smile at, weapons laugh to scorn,
Brandish'd by man that's of a woman born.
[*Exit.*

[*Alarums. Enter* MACDUFF]

MACD. That way the noise is. Tyrant, show thy face!
If thou be'st slain and with no stroke of mine,
My wife and children's ghosts will haunt me still.
I cannot strike at wretched kerns, whose arms
Are hired to bear their staves: either thou, Macbeth,
Or else my sword with an unbatter'd edge
I sheathe again undeeded. There thou shouldst be;
By this great clatter, one of greatest note
Seems bruited. Let me find him, fortune!
And more I beg not.
[*Exit. Alarums.*

[*Enter* MALCOLM *and old* SIWARD.]

16. still, forever. **18. staves,** lances. **20. undeeded,** unused. **22. bruited,**

SIW. This way, my lord; the castle's gently render'd:
The tyrant's people on both sides do fight;
The noble thanes do bravely in the war;
The day almost itself professes yours,
And little is to do.

MAL. We have met with foes
That strike beside us.

SIW. Enter, sir, the castle.
[*Exeunt. Alarums.*

SCENE VIII. *Another part of the field.*

[*Enter* MACBETH.]

MACB. Why should I play the Roman fool, and die
On mine own sword? whiles I see lives, the gashes
Do better upon them.

[*Enter* MACDUFF.]

MACD. Turn, hell-hound, turn!

MACB. Of all men else I have avoided thee:
But get thee back; my soul is too much charged
With blood of thine already.

MACD. I have no words:
My voice is in my sword: thou bloodier villain
Than terms can give thee out! [*They fight.*

MACB. Thou losest labour:
As easy mayst thou the intrenchant air
With thy keen sword impress as make me bleed:
Let fall thy blade on vulnerable crests;
I bear a charmèd life, which must not yield
To one of woman born.

MACD. Despair thy charm;

announced. **24. gently render'd,** tamely surrendered. **27. itself professes,** declares itself. **29. strike beside us,** fight on our side or deliberately avoid striking us. **Scene viii: 1. Roman fool,** allusion to the custom of stoical Roman soldiers of committing suicide to avoid capture. **2. lives,** i.e., any enemies alive. **5. charged,** burdened. **8. terms . . . out,** words can describe thee. **9. intrenchant,** that cannot be cut. **10. impress,** make an impression on. **12. charmed,** protected by

And let the angel whom thou still hast served
Tell thee, Macduff was from his mother's womb
Untimely ripp'd.

MACB. Accursed be that tongue that tells me so,
For it hath cow'd my better part of man!
And be these juggling fiends no more believed,
That palter with us in a double sense;
That keep the word of promise to our ear,
And break it to our hope. I'll not fight with thee.

MACD. Then yield thee, coward
And live to be the show and gaze o' the time:
We'll have thee, as our rarer monsters are,
Painted upon a pole, and underwrit,
"Here may you see the tyrant."

MACB. I will not yield,
To kiss the ground before young Malcolm's feet,
And to be baited with the rabble's curse.
Though Birnam wood be come to Dunsinane,
And thou opposed, being of no woman born,
Yet I will try the last. Before my body
I throw my warlike shield. Lay on, Macduff,
And damn'd be him that first cries "Hold, enough!"

[*Exeunt, fighting. Alarums.*

[*Retreat. Flourish. Enter, with drum and colours,* MALCOLM, *old* SIWARD, ROSS, *the other* THANES, *and* SOLDIERS.]

MAL. I would the friends we miss were safe arrived.

SIW. Some must go off: and yet, by these I see,
So great a day as this is cheaply bought.

MAL. Macduff is missing, and your noble son.

ROSS. Your son, my lord, has paid a soldier's debt:

magic. **14. angel,** here = demon. **18. better . . . man,** i.e., courage. **20. palter,** play false. **24. show . . . time,** an exhibit and spectacle for the public. **26. Painted upon a pole,** i.e., painted on a canvas and put up on a pole (like exhibits before a sideshow at an Elizabethan fair). **29. baited,** attacked on all sides. **32. try the last,** make a final attempt. **33. throw,** hold up. **36. go off,** die; **by,** judging by the number of. **41. which,** i.e., has arrived at man's estate.

He only lived but till he was a man;
The which no sooner had his prowess confirm'd
In the unshrinking station where he fought,
But like a man he died.

SIW. Then he is dead?

ROSS. Ay, and brought off the field: your cause of sorrow
Must not be measured by his worth, for then
It hath no end.

SIW. Had he his hurts before?

ROSS. Ay, on the front.

SIW. Why then, God's soldier be he!
Had I as many sons as I have hairs,
I would not wish them to a fairer death:
And so, his knell is knoll'd.

MAL. He's worth more sorrow,
And that I'll spend for him.

SIW. He's worth no more:
They say he parted well, and paid his score:
And so, God be with him! Here comes newer comfort.

[*Re-enter* MACDUFF, *with* MACBETH'S *head.*]

MACD. Hail, king! for so thou art: behold, where stands
The usuper's cursed head: the time is free:
I see thee compass'd with thy kingdom's pearl,
That speak my salutation in their minds;
Whose voices I desire aloud with mine:
Hail, King of Scotland!

ALL. Hail, King of Scotland! [*Flourish.*

MAL. We shall not spend a large expense of time
Before we reckon with your several loves,
And make us even with you. My thanes and kinsmen,

42. unshrinking station, the post he did not desert. **46. hurts before,** wounds in the front of his body. **50. knoll'd,** tolled. **52. parted well,** died honorably; **score,** bill, i.e., like a guest at an inn. **55. time is free,** this generation is freed (from the tyrant). **56. compass'd . . . pearl,** surrounded by the chief ornaments of your kingdom. **61. reckon . . . loves,** reward the loyalty of each one of you. **66. As,** such as. **68. Producing forth,** bringing to justice.

Henceforth be earls, the first that ever Scotland
In such an honour named. What's more to do,
Which would be planted newly with the time,
As calling home our exiled friends abroad
That fled the snares of watchful tyranny;
Producing forth the cruel ministers
Of this dead butcher and his fiend-like queen,
Who, as 'tis thought, by self and violent hands
Took off her life; this, and what needful else
That calls upon us, by the grace of Grace,
We will perform in measure, time and place:
So, thanks to all at once and to each one,
Whom we invite to see us crown'd at Scone.

[*Flourish. Exeunt.*

66. **As,** such as. 68. **Producing forth,** bringing to justice. 70. **self and violent,** her own violent. 72. **Grace,** i.e., God. 73. **in . . . place,** after due consideration at the proper time and place.

BIBLIOGRAPHY

Bibliography

F. W. Bateson, ed., *The Cambridge Bibliography of English Literature* (Cambridge Univ. Press, 1940), Vol. I. *Supplement,* Vol. V (1957), ed. George Watson.

Gordon Ross Smith, ed., *A Classified Shakespeare Bibliography, 1936-1958* (Pennsylvania State Univ. Press, 1963).

Biography

Joseph Quincy Adams, *A Life of William Shakespeare* (New York 1923).

T. W. Baldwin, *William Shakespere's Small Latine and Lesse Greeke* (Univ. of Illinois Press, 1944), two vols.

G. E. Bentley, *Shakespeare: a Biographical Handbook* (Yale Univ. Press, 1961).

E. K. Chambers, *William Shakespeare: A Study of Facts and Problems* (Oxford Univ. Press, 1930), two vols.

Mark Eccles, *Shakespeare in Warwickshire* (Univ. of Wisconsin Press, 1961).

James G. McManaway, *The Authorship of Shakespeare* (Cornell Univ. Press, 1962).

Textual Problems

W. W. Greg, *The Editorial Problem in Shakespeare* (Oxford Univ. Press, 1954).

____________, *The Shakespeare First Folio: Its Bibliographical and Textual History* (Oxford Univ. Press, 1955).

C. K. Hinman, *The Printing and Proof-Reading of the First Folio of Shakespeare* (Oxford Univ. Press, 1955).

A. W. Pollard, *Shakespeare's Fight with the Pirates and the Problems of the Transmission of His Text* (Cambridge Univ. Press, 1937).

Alice Walker, *Textual Problems of the First Folio* (Cambridge Univ. Press, 1953).

Background

Hardin Craig, *The Enchanted Glass* (Essential Books, 1952).

Walter Raleigh, Sidney Lee, and C. T. Onions, eds., *Shakespeare's England* (Oxford Univ. Press, 1919), two vols.

Theodore Spencer, *Shakespeare and the Nature of Man* (New York, 1942).

E. M. W. Tillyard, *The Elizabethan World Picture* (New York 1943).

Louis B. Wright, *Middle-Class Culture in Elizabethan England* (Univ. of North Carolina Press, 1935).

Theatrical Background

John Cranford Adams, *The Globe Playhouse: Its Design and Equipment* (Harvard Univ. Press, 1942).

T. W. Baldwin, *Organization and Personnel of the Shakespearean Company* (Princeton Univ. Press, 1927).

Bernard Beckerman, *Shakespeare at the Globe, 1599-1609* (New York, 1962).

Muriel C. Bradbrook, *Elizabethan Stage Conditions: A Study of Their Place in the Interpretation of Shakespeare's Plays* (Hamden, Conn., 1962).

E. K. Chambers, *The Elizabethan Stage* (Oxford Univ. Press, 1923), four vols.

Alfred Harbage, *Shakespeare's Audience* (Columbia Univ. Press, 1941).

————, *Shakespeare and the Rival Traditions* (New York, 1952).

C. Walter Hodges, *The Globe Restored* (New York, 1953).

Martin R. Holmes, *Shakespeare's Public: The Touchstone of His Genius* (London, 1960).

B. L. Joseph, *Elizabethan Acting* (Oxford Univ. Press, 1964).

A. M. Nagler, *Shakespeare's Stage* (New Haven, 1958).

Irwin Smith, *Shakespeare's Globe Playhouse* (New York, 1957).

Arthur C. Sprague, *Shakespeare and the Actors, 1660-1905* (New York, 1963).

General Critical Studies

Peter Alexander, *Shakespeare's Life and Art* (London, 1939) .

S. L. Bethell, *Shakespeare and the Popular Dramatic Tradition* (New York, 1944).

A. C. Bradley, *Oxford Lectures on Poetry* (Indiana Univ. Press, 1961).

Joseph A. Bryant, Jr., *Hippolyta's View: Some Christian Aspects of Shakespeare's Plays* (Univ. of Kentucky Press, 1961).

Geoffrey Bullough, ed., *Narrative and Dramatic Sources of Shakespeare* (Columbia Univ. Press, 1957-1964), five vols.

Geoffrey Bush, *Shakespeare and the Natural Condition* (Harvard Univ. Press, 1956).

Oscar J. Campbell, *Shakespeare's Satire* (Oxford Univ. Press, 1943).

Hardin, Craig, *An Interpretation of Shakespeare* (New York, 1948).
W. C. Curry, *Shakespeare's Philosophical Patterns* (Baton Rouge, 1937).
John F. Danby, *Poets on Fortune's Hill* (London, 1952).
Madeleine Doran, *Endeavors of Art: A Study of Form in Elizabethan Drama* (Univ. of Wisconsin Press, 1954).
Henri Fluchère, *Shakespeare and the Elizabethans* (New York 1953).
Harold C. Goddard, *The Meaning of Shakespeare* (Chicago, 1951).
Harley Granville-Barker, *Prefaces to Shakespeare* (Princeton Univ. Press, 1946-47), two vols.
Alfred Harbage, *As They Liked It* (New York, 1947).
Karl Holzknecht, *Backgrounds of Shakespeare's Plays* (New York, 1950).
Frank Kermode, *Four Centuries of Shakespearian Criticism.* (New York: Avon, 1965).
Leo Kirschbaum, *Character and Characterization in Shakespeare* (Wayne State Univ. Press, 1962).
G. Wilson Knight, *The Crown of Life* (London, 1947).
____________, *The Imperial Theme* (London, 1931).
____________, *The Wheel of Fire* (Oxford Univ. Press, 1930).
L. C. Knights, *Explorations* (New York Univ. Press, 1964).
____________, *Some Shakespearean Themes* (Stanford Univ. Press, 1960).
Jan Kott, *Shakespeare, Our Contemporary* (New York, 1964).
Honor Matthews, *Character and Symbol in Shakespeare's Plays: A Study of Certain Christian and Pre-Christian Elements in their Structure and Imagery* (Cambridge, 1962).
Richard G. Moulton, *Shakespeare as Dramatic Artist* (Oxford Univ. Press, 1929).
Allardyce Nicoll, *Shakespeare: An Introduction* (Oxford Univ. Press, 1952).
Arthur Sewell, *Characters and Society in Shakespeare* (Clarendon Press, 1951).
Donald A. Stauffer, *Shakespeare's World of Images* (New York, 1949).
J. I. M. Stewart, *Character and Motive in Shakespeare* (New York, 1949).
E. M. W. Tillyard, *Shakespeare's Problem Plays* (Uiv. of Toronto Press, 1949).
D. A. Traversi, *An Approach to Shakespeare* (London, 1957).
Mark Van Doren, *Shakespeare* (New York, 1939).

General Critical Anthologies

Leonard F. Dean, ed., *Shakespeare: Modern Essays in Criticism* (Oxford Univ. Press, 1957).

Anne B. Ridler, ed., *Shakespeare Criticism,* 1919-1935 (Oxford Univ. Press, 1936).

————, ed., *Shakespeare Criticism,* 1935-1960 (Oxford Univ. Press, 1963).

Paul N. Siegel, ed., *His Infinite Variety: Major Shakespearean Criticism Since Johnson* (Philadelphia, 1964).

D. Nichol Smith, ed., *Shakespeare Criticism, 1623-1840* (Oxford Univ. Press, 1961).

Language Studies

Wolfgang Clemen, *The Development of Shakespeare's Imagery* (Harvard Univ. Press, 1951).

B. Ifor Evans, *The Language of Shakespeare's Plays* (London, 1952).

Hilda M. Hulme, *Explorations in Shakespeare's Language* (London, 1962).

Helge Kokeritz, *Shakespeare's Pronunciation* (Yale Univ. Press, 1953).

M. M. Mahood, *Shakespeare's Wordplay* (London, 1957). Discusses the artistic use of puns in, among other plays, *Macbeth.*

C. T. Onions, *A Shakespeare Glossary* (Oxford Univ. Press, 1953).

Sister Miriam Joseph, *Rhetoric in Shakespeare's Time* (New York, 1962).

Caroline F. E. Spurgeon, *Shakespeare's Imagery and What It Tells Us* (Cambridge Univ. Press, 1952).

Studies in the Tragedies and Specific Studies of Macbeth

A. C. Bradley, *Shakespearean Tragedy* (New York: World Publishing Company, 1961). First published in 1904, this is a classic of Shakespearean criticism, lucid and profound. *Macbeth* chapters deal with characters and atmosphere.

Lily B. Campbell, *Shakespeare's Tragic Heroes, Slaves of Passion* (New York: Barnes and Noble, 1961). The heroes of the great tragedies in the light of Elizabethan psychology. Macbeth wavers between fear and rashness.

H. B. Charlton, *Shakespearian Tragedy* (Cambridge: Cambridge University Press, 1952). Bradleyan criticism. Character analysis and the cultural setting.

Thomas De Quincey, "On the Knocking at the Gate in *Macbeth,*" *Shakespeare Criticism, 1623-1840,* ed. D. Nichol Smith (London: Oxford University Press, 1961). Classic of romantic criticism.

Willard Farnham, *Shakespeare's Tragic Frontier: The World of his Final Tragedies* (Berkeley: University of California Press, 1950). Macbeth as one of Shakespeare's later deeply flawed heroes. Also deals with witchcraft.

Francis Fergusson, "*Macbeth* as the Imitation of an Action," *English Institute Essays* (New York: Columbia University Press, 1952). The governing idea is the violation of nature.

G. Wilson Knight, *The Imperial Theme* (London: Methuen, 1951). Work of an influential symbolist critic. Contains essay on "life-themes" in *Macbeth.*

____________, *The Wheel of Fire* (London: Methuen, 1949). Contains a chapter on the moral darkness of atmosphere.

L. C. Knights, *Explorations* (London: Chatto & Windus, 1946). Contains an essay on *Macbeth,* attacking Bradley's character analysis and analyzing the interplay of themes.

____________, *Some Shakespearean Themes* (Stanford, Calif.: Stanford University Press, 1960). Time and change, appearance and reality, fear of death and fear of life, meanings of nature, etc., in *Macbeth* and other plays.

F. C. Kolbe, *Shakespeare's Way* (London: Sheed & Ward, 1930). The significance of repetitive words in the plays. Antithesis in *Macbeth.*

R. G. Moulton, *Shakespeare as a Dramatic Artist* (Oxford: Clarendon Press, 1888). Plot construction. Dramatic irony in *Macbeth.*

Kenneth Muir, ed., *Macbeth* (New York: Random House ["New Arden" edition, paperback], 1962). Most substantial edition of the play. Contains useful introduction that, among other things, gives survey of nineteenth-century *Macbeth* criticism.

____________, ed., *Shakespeare Survey,* Vol. XIX (Cambridge: Cambridge University Press, 1966). Volume devoted to *Macbeth.* Contains significant studies and useful review of twentieth-century *Macbeth* criticism.

John Middleton Murry, *Shakespeare* (New York: Harcourt, Brace, 1936). Neo-romantic criticism of dramas. Imagery of time in *Macbeth.*

Kenneth O. Myrick, "The Theme of Damnation in Shakespearean Tragedy" (*Studies in Philology,* XXXVIII, 1941). Guilt, repentance, and damnation in *Hamlet, Macbeth,* and *Othello.*

Arthur Quiller-Couch, *Shakespeare's Workmanship* (Cambridge: Cambridge University Press, 1931). Lectures on dramas. Morality play influence and Macbeth as criminal-hero.

Irving Ribner, *Patterns in Shakespearean Tragedy* (London: Methuen, 1960). *Macbeth* and other tragedies in relation to Shakespeare's inherited ideas and dramatic forms.

L. L. Shücking, *Character Problems in Shakespeare's Plays* (New York: Holt, 1922). Dramatic conventions in characterization. Macbeth essentially ignoble.

Paul N. Siegel, *Shakespearean Tragedy and the Elizabethan Compromise* (New York: New York University Press, 1957). Shakespearean tragedy in relation to contemporary social and intellectual changes. Two opposing views of manhood in *Macbeth.*

Robert Speaight, *Nature in Shakespearean Tragedy* (London: Hollis & Carter, 1955). Nature and Grace in *Macbeth* and other tragedies.

Theodore Spencer, *Shakespeare and the Nature of Man* (New York: Macmillan Company, 1949). Survey of dramas, including *Macbeth,* in relation to Elizabethan world-picture.

Caroline Spurgeon, "Shakespeare's Iterative Imagery," *Studies in Shakespeare: British Academy Lectures,* ed. Peter Alexander, 1964. Running images in *Macbeth* and other tragedies.

J. I. M. Stewart, *Character and Motive in Shakespeare* (New York: Longmans, Green, 1949). Shakespeare's characters in light of twentieth-century psychology. Seeming inconsistencies in Macbeth as psychologically accurate.

Brents Stirling, *Unity in Shakespearean Tragedy: The Interplay of Theme and Character* (New York: Columbia University Press, 1957). Leading ideas in relation to structure and motivation. Themes of "raptness" and inverted nature in *Macbeth.*

E. M. W. Tillyard, *Shakespeare's History Plays* (New York: Macmillan Company, 1946). *Macbeth* in relation to the history plays and Elizabethan political thought.

D. A. Traversi, *Approach to Shakespeare* (London: Sands, 1957). Close analysis of language and verse of dramas. "Degree" in *Macbeth.*

Mark Van Doren, *Shakespeare* (New York: Holt, 1939). Brief, perceptive essays. Time and atmosphere in *Macbeth.*

Roy Walker, *The Time is Free* (London: Dakers, 1949). Book-length study of *Macbeth.* Imagery, irony, and the tragic pattern.

GLOSSARY-INDEX

Proper Names, Critical Terms, Images, Themes*

* This index of significant images, themes, and uses of dramatic irony referred to in the "Commentary" of the COMPREHENSIVE SUMMARY is not intended to be an exhaustive listing of the occurrences of the items in the play, as it was not thought advisable to include each such item in the "Commentary." The theme of the difference between appearance and reality, for example, appears in various forms in the play, and the student may wish to explore other instances of it than those listed here.

Cawdor, Thane of—traitor in the battle of Act I, his title is awarded Macbeth; see COMPREHENSIVE SUMMARY, "Commentary" on I,ii,45-67.

choric—refers to a character who, like the chorus in Greek tragedy, comments upon the action, generalizing upon it and serving as a guide to the response of the audience. Also, refers to a speech which serves this function. See Comprehensive Summary, "Commentary" on II,iv,1-20; and CHARACTER ANALYSES, "The Other Characters."

clothing, imagery of—see COMPREHENSIVE SUMMARY, especially "Commentary" on I,iii,89-156; V,ii.

comic relief—relief through comedy from the tension of a drama for the purpose of loosening a strain which may otherwise become too intense. Slackening the tension enables it to be built up again. Comic relief is only one way of relieving tension (see *pathos*, below), but in Shakespeare comic relief has a thematic relationship to the tragedy. See, for example, "Commentary" on the Porter scene, II,iii,1-47 in the COMPREHENSIVE SUMMARY.

darkness, imagery of—see COMPREHENSIVE SUMMARY, "Commentary" on I,i; I,iv,48-58; I,v,31-55; II,i,1-32; II,iv,1-20; III,ii,1-56; III,iii,1-24; IV,iii,159-240. See, also, STUDY QUESTIONS, 2.

disease, imagery of—see COMPREHENSIVE SUMMARY, "Commentary" on III,ii,1-56; III,iv,1-32; IV,ii,1-29; IV,iii,139-159; V,i; V,ii and iii. See, also, STUDY QUESTIONS, 3.

disorder, imagery of—see COMPREHENSIVE SUMMARY, "Commentary" on I,i; II,iii,48-68; III,iv,1-32; III,ii,1-56; IV,I,1-47; IV,ii,1-29; IV,iii,1-139; V,ii.

Donalbain—son of Duncan.

Duncan—see, especially, CHARACTER ANALYSES.

Dunsinane—Macbeth's royal stronghold of Act V; see KEY MAP, p. 4.

Elizabeth—see COMPLETE BACKGROUND, "Shakespeare's England—Religious Atmosphere," "—Political Milieu."

exposition—the means by which the dramatist imparts to the audience the necessary facts concerning the initial situation. How he is to do this while arousing interest is a technical problem. Shakespeare often, as in *Macbeth*, begins with a highly dramatic scene and then, the attention of the audience having been gained, engages in the exposition. See *Macdonwald*, below.

fertility, imagery of—see COMPREHENSIVE SUMMARY, "Commentary" on I,iv,1-47; I,vi,1-10; III,i,44-72; IV,i,135-156; IV,ii,65-85; V,ix.

flat character—a character in literature with a dominant trait on which the author has so focussed that the character does not give the impression of a rounded personality: he is two- rather than three-dimensional. Such a flat character may serve an artistic purpose, as for instance, when the author wishes the representativeness of the character to be stressed to gain universality. Thus Lady Macbeth's gentlewoman represents simple, ordinary humanity awed by the revelation of Lady Macbeth's tortured soul.

Fleance—son of Banquo, he escapes murder in III,iii that Banquo's line might continue unbroken.

Folios, discussion of—see WILLIAM SHAKESPEARE, "Shakespeare's Writings—Order of Publication."

Forres—site of Duncan's palace; see KEY MAP, p. 4.

Glamis, Thane of—Macbeth's title as the drama opens.

Gunpowder Plot—see COMPLETE BACKGROUND, "Shakespeare's England—Contemporary Events," and "Introduction to the Play—Topicality"; also see COMPREHENSIVE SUMMARY, "Commentary" on II,iii,1-43.

Hecate—see COMPLETE BACKGROUND, "Introduction to the Play—The Witches"; also COMPREHENSIVE SUMMARY, III,v, and IV,i.

Henry VIII—see COMPLETE BACKGROUND, "Shakespeare's England—Religious Atmosphere," "—Political Milieu."

Holinshed's Chronicles—see COMPLETE BACKGROUND, "Introduction to the Play—Sources," "—The Witches."

image—not merely a word-picture but any sense-impression—that of sound, smell, and taste as well as sight—evoked by words used either literally or figuratively. The same group of words may evoke many sense-impressions and be classified in different ways in the study of patterns of images. "He cannot buckle his distemper'd cause/ Within the belt of rule" may be called a clothing image (picture of a man trying to buckle his belt). a disease image (picture of a man whose waist is swollen by dropsy [the meaning of *distemper'd*]), and a disorder image (the idea of a lack of control indicated by the inability of the belt to girdle the waist).

Inverness—Macbeth's castle; see COMPREHENSIVE SUMMARY, "Commentary" on I,vi,1-10; see, also, KEY MAP, p. 4.

irony, dramatic—the audience's perception, either at the time or later, that the words uttered by a speaker have a meaning other than that which either he or the listener or both realize. Also, the audience's perception that a character's action has had an entirely different effect from that which he intended. Dramatic irony, then, is a result of the ignorance of characters. In tragedy dramatic irony creates a sense of the blindness of human beings concerning reality, a blindness that brings about calamity. See COMPREHENSIVE SUMMARY, "Commentary" on I,iii,1-37; I,iv,1-47; I,iv,48-58; I,vi,1-10; I,vii, 1-28; II,i,1-32; II,ii,14-57; II,iii,1-47; II,iii,48-68; II,iii,69-101 III,i,44-72; III,ii,1-56; IV,ii,30-64; V,i and v. See, also, STUDY QUESTIONS, 1.

James I—see COMPLETE BACKGROUND, "Shakespeare's England—Political Milieu," and "Introduction to the Play—Topicality." See, also, COMPREHENSIVE SUMMARY, "Commentary" on IV,i,48-135.

Lady Macbeth—see, especially, CHARACTER ANALYSES.

Lady Macduff—see, especially, COMPREHENSIVE SUMMARY, "Commentary" on iv,ii.

Lennox—Scotch lord; see COMPREHENSIVE SUMMMARY, *passim.*

Macbeth—see CHARACTER ANALYSES; CRITICAL ANALYSIS, throughout; and COMPREHENSIVE SUMMARY, *passim.*

Macdonwald—rebel slain by Macbeth as narrated by the captain in the exposition of I,ii.

Macduff—see, especially, *Character Analyses.*

Malcolm—Scotch lord and original heir to Duncan's throne; see, especially, CHARACTER ANALYSES.

manliness, theme of—see COMPREHENSIVE SUMMARY, "Commentary" on I,vii,28-82; II,ii,14-57; III,i,73-142; III,iv,32-121; III,iv, 122-144; IV,iii,159-240; V,v and ix. See, also, STUDY QUESTIONS, 4.

Menteith—Scotch lord; see COMPREHENSIVE SUMMARY, V,ii.

milk, imagery of—see COMPREHENSIVE SUMMARY, "Commentary" on I,v,31-55; IV,iii,1-139.

Murderers, the—see COMPREHENSIVE SUMMARY, "Commentary" on III,i,73-142; III,iii; IV,ii,65-85.

natural order, theme of—see COMPREHENSIVE SUMMARY, "Commentary" on I,i; I,iii,89-156; I,iv,1-47; I,v,31-55; I,vi,1-10; I,vii,1-28; I,vii,28-82; II,i,1-32; II,i,33-64; II,iii,1-47; II,iii,48-68;

II,iv,1-20; III,i,73-142; III,ii,1-56; IV,i,1-47; IV,ii,1-29; V,i and v.

Old Man, the—see COMPREHENSIVE SUMMARY, "Commentary" on II,iv,1-20; also see *choric*, above.

pathos—the quality in literature which arouses the feeling of pity. Fear and pity are the dominant feelings aroused by tragedy. We experience fear in the face of the impending misfortune of a character with whom we identify ourselves or in the face of an impending or actual misfortune of a character whom we perceive to be representative of humanity. We experience pity on regarding helpless or unmerited suffering. A scene of *pathos* may act as relief from tension by releasing our feelings.

Physician, the—see COMPREHENSIVE SUMMARY, "Commentary" on V,i.

Porter, the—see COMPREHENSIVE SUMMARY, "Commentary" on II,iii, 1-47.

quartos, discussion of—see WILLIAM SHAKESPEARE, "Shakespeare's Writings—Order of Publication."

reversal of values, theme of—see COMPREHENSIVE SUMMARY, "Commentary" on I,i; I,v,1-31; III,i,73-142; IV,iii,1-139; V,vi.

Ross, Thane of—see COMPREHENSIVE SUMMARY, I,ii; I,iii; II,iv; and *passim.*

Scone—scene of Macbeth's coronation; see COMPREHENSIVE SUMMARY, II,iv; also KEY MAP, p. 4.

setting—the physical and spiritual background of the drama. In the modern theater, the scenery contributes to the sense of setting, but the Elizabethan theater did not have any elaborate scenery (see p. 8), and the dramatist appealed to the audience's imagination through the poetry. The setting of *Macbeth* includes the darkness of the night-scenes, indicated in the dialogue and through the stage-properties of torches and candles, the gloomy castles with heavily barred gates and alarum-bells, the sense of a time of early feudalism in which social stability is precarious and bloodshed common.

Siward—aged British general; see COMPREHENSIVE SUMMARY, V,ii and vii. See, also, *Young Siward,* below.

symbol—that which in addition to being itself comes, as a result of the context in which it appears, to stand for or represent something else. This may be an image, an action, or a sight visible on the stage. Thus milk stands for compassion, tenderness, and natural human feelings. These are suggested by Lady Macbeth's words about "the milk o' human kindness" as well as by the conventional ideas of the day.

theme—an idea or motif which recurs and is developed in different ways. Also, the general idea which emerges from the whole work.

turning-point—the point from which the forces opposing the hero start to gain the ascendancy which will cause his final defeat.

uncertainty, theme of—see COMPREHENSIVE SUMMARY, "Commentary" on I,iii,38-88; III,iii,1-24; IV,ii,1-29; IV,iii,1-139.

Witches, the—see COMPLETE BACKGROUND, "Introduction to the Play"; COMPREHENSIVE SUMMARY, "Commentary" on I,i; I,iii,1-37; III,v; IV,i,1-47.

Young Siward—son of the English general; see COMPREHENSIVE SUMMARY, V,vii.